BACKWARD, CHRISTIAN SOLDIERS?

Other books by Gary North

Marx's Religion of Revolution, 1968
An Introduction to Christian Economics, 1973
Unconditional Surrender, 1981
Successful Investing in an Age of Envy, 1981
The Dominion Covenant: Genesis, 1982
Government By Emergency, 1983
The Last Train Out, 1983
*75 Bible Questions Your Instructors
    Pray You Won't Ask*, 1984
*Coined Freedom: Gold in the Age of
    the Bureaucrats*, 1984
Moses and Pharaoh, 1985
Negatrends, 1985
The Sinai Strategy, 1986
*Unholy Spirits: Occultism and
    New Age Humanism*, 1986
Conspiracy: A Biblical View, 1986
Honest Money, 1986
Inherit the Earth, 1986

Books Edited by Gary North

Foundations of Christian Scholarship, 1976
Tactics of Christian Resistance, 1983
The Theology of Christian Resistance, 1983

BACKWARD, CHRISTIAN SOLDIERS?

An Action Manual for Christian Reconstruction

Gary North

Institute for Christian Economics
Tyler, Texas

Published by
Institute for Christian Economics
P.O. Box 8000
Tyler, Texas 75711

This book is dedicated to

Gen. Albion Knight

who has honorably worn
the uniforms of two armies,
Christ's and the
United States Army's.

TABLE OF CONTENTS

INTRODUCTION

"This little book introduces Christians to a new way of thinking about the world around them—a positive, optimistic way of thinking."

This little book is about victory. Not just victory over indwelling sin in each regenerate person's heart, but victory over the effects of sin in every area of life. It can be done. Not perfectly, of course. Perfect victory over personal sin comes only on the day of a person's death, or on the day of resurrection, whichever comes first. Perfect victory over the effects of sin throughout the universe comes only at the day of judgment. But progressive victory over sin in the individual's life can and should be mirrored in the progressive victory over the effects of sin in the society. This is the message of Deuteronomy 8 and 28:1-14.

Christians haven't taken seriously this vision of victory since the 1870's. They have become convinced that the best we can hope for is *individual sanctification*. They have rejected the concept of *social sanctification*. What is personal sanctification, anyway? It is the progressive conformity of a person's life to the standards set forth by the Bible for ethics. It means becoming conformed to the perfect humanity of Christ. (It never means becoming conformed to His divinity; men do not evolve into God.) Sanctification is a process of being *set apart* from the world of sin and ethical rebellion — again, not perfectly, in time and on earth, but progressively. Regenerate men become "meat eaters" rather than "milk drinkers" (I Cor 3:2).

Then what is social sanctification? It parallels personal sanctification. As godly people begin to restructure their behavior in terms of what the Bible requires, the world about them begins to change. They serve as leavening influences in the whole culture. As more converts are added to the rolls of the churches, and as these converts begin to conform their lives to the Bible's standards for external behavior, all of society is progressively sanctified — set apart by God for His glory, just as He set apart Israel in Old Testament times.

What I try to show in this book is that the vision of victory that God gave to Abram when he was still without a son, and that He gave Moses before he confronted Pharaoh, and that Christ announced after His resurrection (Matt. 28:18) is still valid. It should still motivate His people to present themselves as a living sacrifice (Rom. 12:1). But for over a century, this vision faded in the hearts and minds of regenerate people. A *vision of defeat*, in time and on earth, replaced the older vision of victory. The churches went into hiding, culturally speaking. They left the battlefield. The humanists won by default.

Since 1980, however, a change has begun to take place. Ministries that previously were uninvolved in social and political affairs have begun to mobilize opposition to abortion, secular humanism in the public schools, and various Federal welfare programs that encourage sexual immorality. Their leaders have begun to use the language of victory, in stark contrast to the cultural pessimism of books like Hal Lindsey's *Late, Great Planet Earth.*

Newer ministries, such as the Maranatha campus evangelism organization (headquartered in Gainesville, Florida), are forthrightly proclaiming the "crown rights of King Jesus" over every area of life. Students associated with Maranatha are bold in challenging humanism on the campus. They see that God calls His people to exercise *dominion* (Gen. 1:28), in time and on earth, as His representatives and ambassadors. The outlook of these students is far different from that of students in the 1950's through the 1970's who were associated with other campus ministries. In those earlier days, almost all the efforts of these organizations were evangelical in the narrow sense: saving men *out of* the world, but not training redeemed men to take responsibility *over* the world.

As I write this introduction in the opening month of 1984, I am struck by the anomaly of three separate

Christian ministries' attempting to establish Christian law schools. For decades, the leaders of these ministries, along with virtually all other conservative Christian leaders, opposed the idea that Christians have a moral responsibility to proclaim an exclusively Christian world-and-life view for the governing of all human institutions. They consciously asserted that "we're under grace, not law."

But then the secular humanists finally opened fire on Christian organizations. Christian leaders discovered that their millions of converts had taken them seriously. These converts had not rethought the legal foundations of American freedom. They did not go to law school and become self-consciously Christian lawyers. So today these ministries are having great difficulty in finding enough faculty members to establish a single new law school, let alone three, and not one legal theorist who comes forth ready to explain the details of an explicitly Bible-based law code. Yet R. J. Rushdoony's *Institutes of Biblical Law* was published in 1973, giving these ministries enough time to have trained up an army of young Christian lawyers. But the leaders of today's besieged ministries did not believe Rushdoony's message in 1973, the same year that the U.S. Supreme Court handed down the infamous *Roe v. Wade* decision which legalized abortion on demand in the United States.

Christians are now playing catch-up, the game the humanists played in this nation from at least 1800. The humanists finally caught up. Then they overtook the Christians. They have gained sufficient control over the media, the public schools, and the seats of power, so that they think they can coerce Christians into compliance to the religion of secular humanism. A handful of Christians have begun to resist, but not many. The escalation of the Christians' confrontation with government bureaucracies has only just begun. (See my essay, "The Escalating Confrontation with Bureaucracy," in *Tactics of Christian Resistance*, issue 3 of *Christianity and Civilization*, 708 Hamvasy Ln., Tyler, TX 75701: $14.95.)

This little book introduces Christians to a new way of thinking about the world around them—a positive, optimistic way of thinking. The book's chapters originally appeared in various newsletters published by the Institute for Christian Economics (P.O. Box 8000, Tyler, TX 75711): *Christian Reconstruction*, *Biblical Economics Today*, and *Dominion Strategies*. Those readers who become convinced by this book should sign up for a free six-month subscription to all I.C.E. publications. Use the tear-out order blank at the back of this book.

1

BACKWARD, CHRISTIAN SOLDIERS?

"Christians believe today that they can safely retreat into a zone of social impotence and therefore social irresponsibility, just as they have done for over a century."

What would you do if a topless bar-adult theater complex opened across the street from your church or Christian school? If your community were hit with a wave of pornographic materials, which institution should take the lead in campaigning against it? A hundred years ago, the answer would have been instantaneous: the local church. Yet when confronted with just this question by members of one southern California conservative church, the pastor replied that the church should do nothing officially. "We can't get involved in social action projects," he said.

"Ye are the salt of the earth: but if the salt have lost his savor, wherewith shall it be salted? It is thenceforth good for nothing, but to be cast out, and to be trodden under foot of men" (Matt. 5:13). Christians have been losing their cultural savor for well over two centuries, and with increasing speed since the end of the Civil War. How could this have happened?

In the twelfth and thirteenth centuries, Christians invented the university, one of the greatest engines of social advancement and cultural enrichment ever conceived. Now they build backwater Bible colleges that send the students to the local secular college or university for the "neutral" academic subjects—like Freudian psychology, Keynesian economics, and evolutionary anthropology. Christian professors offer no explicitly biblical alternatives to their students.

CHALLENGING A WHOLE CULTURE The Reformation saw the advent of modern printing, and the bulk of that printing was Christian, and by no means limited to gushy devotional tracts. Luther was challenging the whole fabric of Western culture; Calvin was rebuilding his city of Geneva (at the desperate request of the local town leaders); John Knox was winning Scotland to the gospel, using the sword as well as the pen. This literature still survives, even in secular college classrooms; it changed our world. The King James Bible established a standard of excellence in the English language that has never been surpassed. Try to find a modern example of Christian literature that has had this kind of impact!

In 1974, I sent the manuscript of *Foundations of*

Christian Scholarship to a Christian publishing firm in Britain. The book's essays challenge the established secular presuppositions of many academic disciplines: economics, sociology, psychology, education, philosophy, political science, and even mathematics. The writers all had advanced degrees, and most held the Ph.D.

The letter of rejection explained that the publishing organization "has been generally very wary about involving itself in this field. There is no one of any real competence to get involved in these matters of economics, sociology, etc. [presumably, he means nobody associated with his publishing firm] and it would be sticking our neck out with no one able to answer the charges that might be made. We see the first concern to address ourselves to the prevailing piety in worship, prayer and preaching. . . ."

THE PROPHETS' LEGACY   What has become of the legacy of the Hebrew prophets, who called a rebellious people — including priests and kings — to repentance and reform? What has become of the whole counsel of God? Why do Christians feel incompetent "to answer the charges that might be made"?

How many times have Bible teachers told their listeners that "the Bible has the answers for all of life's problems"? The statement is true, of course, and what we know as Western Civilization was built upon this truth. Yet the moment Christians discover answers in the Bible to the many problems of life that lie outside the narrow confines of the institutional church, they feel impotent and unqualified to speak.

Christians feel themselves helpless in the face of the complexity of life and the massed intellectual troops of modern secularism. A friend of mine, whose training was in natural science and who was once employed as an analyst of "war games" in a scientific think-tank, commented twenty years ago: "It's ironic. Christians look at science and see a roaring lion, when it's really a mouse in the corner, shivering."

Like ten of the twelve spies sent out by Moses to report on the military capacities of the various Canaanitic cultures (Num. 13), our reports are filled with dismay. Yet Rahab was to tell the spies of the next generation that "as soon as we heard these things, our hearts did melt, neither did there remain any more courage in any man, because of you: for the LORD your God, he is God in heaven above, and in earth beneath" (Josh. 2:11).

Lord in the earth beneath: here is the battle cry of faithful Christians in every generation. Not Lord in the heaven above, but impotent on earth, but Lord of heaven and earth. The misinterpretation of Christ's words — that His kingdom is not of this world — should finally be given the burial it deserves. He was asserting to Pilate that His *source* of authority and lordship was not an earthly source, but a heavenly source. His words are clear: "if my kingdom were of this world, then would my servants fight, that I should not be delivered to the Jews: but now is my kingdom not from hence" (John 18:36). Not *from* hence: He was speaking of the *source* of His authority, not the place of His legitimate reign. His kingdom is not *of* this world but it *is* in this world and over it.

But how many retreatist sermons have been preached concerning the solely spiritual, exclusively internal realm of Christ's kingdom, as a supposedly accurate explanation of this famous biblical text? I shudder to think of the number: like the sands of the sea shore.

CHRISTIAN SCHOLARSHIP Why should Christians be afraid to challenge the secular culture of today? Has there ever been a culture less sure of its own beliefs, less confident of its own powers, more confused concerning its own destiny? The newspapers, the entertainment media, and the universities can speak of little else but defeat and alienation. When a rare piece of positive drama appears, it usually deals with some historical figure, like Patton or Cromwell. The Christians have hardly heard of Cromwell, the great Puritan leader and revolutionary general. Secularists such as the author Antonia Fraser or the producers of "Cromwell" have to remind modern Christians of their own heritage, so forgetful have orthodox believers become. We let the secularists do even our spiritual work for us, so debilitating have been the effects of emotional, pietistic withdrawal.

Why should critiques of modern secularism be left to neo-orthodox scholars like the theologian Langdon Gilkey, whose book, *Maker of Heaven and Earth* (at least in the first six chapters), was for years the best book available on the implications of the doctrine of God's creation—something Gilkey does not even believe in its historic form? Why was it left to him to remind Christians that without the sure foundation of the belief in the creation, modern science could never have arisen? He, not the local pastor, has announced: "The optimism and buoyancy of Western culture is more an effect of the idea of the good creation than its cause."

With the fading belief in the creation, we have seen the coming of major intellectual crises in science and the arts. Who has informed modern Christians that without permanent standards of law and truth, no progress or development is possible, and that with the coming of relativism we have seen the death of the idea of optimistic progress? Why can't it be some internationally known evangelist rather than a secularist like Gunther Stent, professor of biology at the University of California, Berkeley? His book, setting forth this idea, *The Coming of the Golden Age: A View of the End of Progress* (1969), was published for the American Museum of Natural History. Why must the secularists do our work?

When we think of Christian scholarship, what do we have in mind? A seminary? But seminaries limit their efforts to instruction in the biblical languages, evangelism, church history, or "practical" theology — counselling, church budgets, visitation, etc. Apart from the Wycliffe translation program, there is hardly a single explicitly Christian endeavor that has impressed the secular world with its competence. We are second rate, or third rate, and we know it. Why? I contend that it is directly related to our stubborn unwillingness to consider the whole counsel of God. A book like R. J. Rushdoony's *Institutes of Biblical*

Law (1973) should have been written two centuries ago; a culture should have flowered because of it. Instead, we let the secularists do our work for us. We do not trust our own competence.

Christians believe today that they can safely retreat into a zone of social impotence and therefore social irresponsibility, just as they have done for a century. But with the acids of relativism and nihilism eroding the foundations of secularism—the faith which has supported the Western world since at least 1900—the social buffers are disappearing. Drugs, pornography, lawlessness, economic disruption, witchcraft, random murders, and all the rest of secularism's new children no longer respect the doors of the churches the way they used to. Like Joab, contemporary Christians are discovering that the horns of the altar no longer protect them from destruction (I Kings 2:28-34). They can no longer be "rice Christians," the beneficiaries of endless fruits of a once-Christian culture.

CONCLUSION Christianity can permanently reconstruct the culture; nothing else can. Secularism is at the end of the road spiritually; nothing is left to hold society together except brute force. God calls His people to leave the onions of Egypt behind them. There are no more safety zones in the war between the faiths. The battle rages. We can no longer whine, like Moses: "O my Lord, I am not eloquent, neither heretofore, nor since thou hast spoken unto thy servant: but I am slow of speech, and of a slow tongue. And the LORD said unto him, Who hath made man's mouth? or who maketh the dumb, or deaf, or the seeing, or the blind? have not I—the LORD? . . . And the anger of the LORD was kindled against Moses . . ." (Ex. 4:10, 11, 14a).

Moses finally had to do what he was told. He took up the challenge God had set before him. He would have saved himself a lot of agony had he responded initially. If it was true for Moses, before the revelation of Jesus Christ, to whom all power has been given (Matt. 28:18), it should be far more true of His New Testament people. The enemy is at the gates.

[This was published in 1974 in the now-defunct magazine, *Applied Christianity*. Since the late 1970's, a resurgence of interest in applied Christianity has begun to be evident. The magazine, however, ceased publication in 1975.]

2

IMPENDING JUDGMENT

"How long do we expect God to withhold His wrath, if by crushing the humanists who promote mass abortion . . . He might spare the lives of literally millions of innocents?"

In recent years, a sense of foreboding has begun to overtake the West. The optimism of the "can-do" pragmatic liberals of the Kennedy years died in the jungles of Vietnam. What has replaced the older optimism is a kind of secularized version of "eat, drink, and be merry, for tomorrow we die." Can-do liberalism couldn't, and its spiritual heirs have just about gone through their inheritance. (Liberalism taxes all kinds of capital, not just financial capital, and the result is national decapitalization.)

There are several ways men have accommodated themselves to this sense of impending doom. One way is to deny the darkness. Men point to statistical indicators of national economic growth, or some other measure of prosperity, and they conclude that things are doing pretty well, so there is no cause for alarm. Ben Wattenberg's recent books are examples of this. Then there is the "imminent return" syndrome among religious groups, especially American Protestants. Jesus is supposedly coming soon, and all these dark signs are like holes in a sinking ship. We Christians have the lifeboats, however. Jesus will deliver us out of our misery. Another approach is the "end of civilization" syndrome. These people are the true pessimists. They see the end of the industrialized West, the coming of repressive barbarism (Chinese, Russian, or home-grown), and the collapse of the modern economy. Finally, we have the "clean sweep" advocates: the crisis will destroy my group's enemies, and my group will be found on top when the dust, however radioactive it may be in the interim, finally settles.

Any of these syndromes is conceivably correct in its conclusions. What we should expect, however, is that there will be more than one scenario (unless Jesus really does come to bail out the Christians). There is a big world out there, and many historical currents are operating. There are many possibilities open to the human race, some bad and some good.

At some point — or better, series of points — affairs come to a head. The direction of events becomes apparent. Alert observers in 1910-14 predicted the coming of a European war, and finally their fears were confirmed. The devastation that struck Europe in 1914-18 was inconceivable even to pessimists in 1913. The face of the world was permanently altered.

Whole cultures disintegrated, and the rise of Bolshevism and Nazism brought decades of additional devastation. We still live under the shadow of that great war. Yet not everything was lost. Not all signs of progress ceased. Men forged ahead, especially in the area of technology. But, on the other hand, there is the hydrogen bomb, technology's highly efficient threat to the world of technology. And what if technology gets the cost of producing such a weapon down to the level where an Idi Amin can buy or steal one?

The prophets of doom and the prophets of continuing progress can both look plausible for a while. There will come a time in the life of any given nation or culture, however, when the implications of its historical development become sufficiently obvious, so that the majority of men can see them. When civilizations fall, men wail the loss, but they recognize it. Even when the fall of a civilization takes centuries, as it did in Rome, the later citizens can look back and recognize the world they have lost. We cannot put off the day of cultural reckoning forever. For a man heavily invested on margin in the U.S. stock market in October of 1929, the day of accounting could not be delayed any longer. What resulted from that collapse (i.e., the depression which began before October 1929, but had not been obvious) was understood as a disaster by those living in the 1930's. The pessimists of the late 1920's were proven correct; the optimists were proven bankrupt.

PROPHETIC PREACHING The prophets of the Old Testament believed that there is a fixed relationship between the moral character of a nation and the external blessings or cursings visited by God on that nation. They believed in the reliability of biblical law. They knew that if people continue to cheat their neighbors, commit adultery, break up the family, and defy all lawfully constituted authorities, the land will be brought under judgment. They had no doubts in this regard. They recapitulated the teachings of Deuteronomy 28:15-68, warning their listeners that God's laws cannot be violated with impunity forever.

Twentieth-century preaching has neglected the outline of Deuteronomy 28. We find few pastors who are willing to stick their necks out and warn congregations that modern society faces the same sort of judgment that faced ancient Israel. They are unwilling to follow the logic of the covenant, namely, that *similar sins result in similar judgments*. While today's religious leaders are sometimes willing to speak of the impending judgment of God on the lawless members of society—a society from which all Christians will have been removed by a supernatural act of God—they are seldom ready to preach as the prophets did. They do not warn their listeners, as Jeremiah did, that they, too, are a part of contemporary society, and that they, too, are not immunized against God's wrath. If men have relied on the continuing profitability of today's economy, and the continuing functioning of today's bureaucratic structures, then they have put their capital at risk. They have rested on, and continue to rest on, weak reeds.

Where is the warning being sounded? Where are

the congregations, let alone denominations, that are being alerted to the risks associated with cultural and economic collapse? Europe has suffered two great wars, several inflations, plus the pressures of Communist revolution, all since 1914. We have seen whole empires decimated in this century, whole peoples engulfed and destroyed—not just in the so-called Third World (Cambodia, for example), but in the civilized West. Yet the pastors in the United States, Canada, and other previously unscathed nations seem to believe that their societies possess some sort of theological "King's X," just because God has spared them in the past. The barbarians are at the gates, threatening the West with destruction, yet the overwhelming majority of pastors have not begun to alert their congregations of the need for prayer, national repentance, Christian reconstruction, and preparation for national disaster. They apparently do not believe that the law-order which prevailed in the Old Testament still has any effect. They do not recognize the threat, for example, of the magnitude of abortions worldwide: between 45 million and 55 million annually. In the United States, the figure is conservatively estimated at a million and a half a year. How long do we expect God to withhold His wrath, if by crushing the humanists who promote mass abortion (including certain faculty members in supposedly orthodox seminaries), He might spare the lives of literally millions of innocents? Will God hesitate to bring us low, just because we have grown accustomed to indoor plumbing and central air conditioning, in the face of mass murder?

The threat of judgment is spelled out clearly in Deuteronomy 28. The reality of judgment has been with us since 1914. The Soviet Union — the most consistent humanist regime in history — has escalated its pressures on the West, and since 1982 has been in a position to launch a successful first strike against America's undefended missiles. Yet any pastor who would dare to mention the wisdom of buying dehydrated food, gold coins, and a home in a small town would be branded as an extremist. What is an extremist? A prophet. And you know what respectable priests and rulers did to the prophets.

CONCLUSION If you are a pastor, and you don't think your congregation wants to hear this kind of message, think about forming a new congregation. It won't be difficult. Just start preaching like a prophet of God, and the losers will leave, or toss you out. Your income as a pastor is going to wipe you out anyway; better seek alternative income now, while you have the opportunity.

If you are a layman, and your pastor refuses to preach like a prophet, find a new church, or do what you can to get a new pastor. Being surrounded by Christian lemmings (grasshoppers, in Aesop's fable) when the crisis hits will be unpleasant. You will need friends who are better prepared than lemmings in that dark day.

3

ESCHATOLOGIES OF SHIPWRECK

> "The State needs pastors who preach a theology of defeat. It keeps the laymen quiet, in an era in which Christian laymen are the most significant potential threat to the unwarranted expansion of state power."

The great chapter in the New Testament which deals with the division of labor within the church is I Corinthians 12. The basic teaching is found in verse 12: "For as the body is one, and hath many members, and all the members of that one body, being many, are one body: so also is Christ." The church, the body of Christ, is to perform as a disciplined, integrated body performs. It is not to fight against itself, trip itself, or be marked by jealousy, one member against another.

The twentieth century has brought with it a deplorable application of these words. Instead of viewing the body of Christ as a symbolic body with

Christ as the head, modern Christians have adopted the Roman Catholic practice of regarding the priesthood as the head, heart, and hands, with laymen serving as the back, feet, and legs. In other words, the priests serve as the unquestioned "specialists in religion," while laymen, including elders, serve as the "secular" hewers of wood and drawers of water. The laymen are specialists in the things of "the world," while their priests take care of the spiritual realm. We call this outlook "sacerdotalism."

This unfortunate development began very early in the history of Protestantism, though its full implications have taken several centuries to work out in practice. Protestant sacerdotalism, like Protestant scholasticism, has been with us for a long time. Laymen have automatically assumed that the division of labor spoken of in the New Testament is a division of labor between secular and spiritual pursuits. But this is not what the New Testament teaches. The New Testament's vision of Christ's comprehensive kingdom involves the whole world. Jesus announced: "All power is given unto me in heaven and in earth" (Matt. 28:18). Modern Christians really cannot seem to accept Christ's words. They reinterpret them to say: "All power is given to me in heaven, but I have abdicated as far as the earth is concerned." The priests, as representatives of Christ's spiritual power, which is supposedly the only real power that Christ systematically exercises, are understood to be the central figures in the kingdom. Laymen, who supposedly specialize in earthly affairs, are bearers of an inferior authority (not merely subordinate authority, but by nature inferior).

One of the reasons why Christians have adopted the peculiar view of authority outlined above has to do with the concept of victory. From Augustine to Kuyper, or from Luther to Barth, expositors have too often limited the promise of victory to the institutional church, or even more radically, to the human heart alone. Where a man's heart is, there will be his kingdom. If his hope of victory is limited to his heart, then his concern will be drastically narrowed. He will worry about his heart, his personal standing before God, his own sanctification, and his relationship to the institutional church. He will be far less concerned about exercising disciplined authority in the so-called secular realm. It is difficult psychologically to wage war on a battlefield which by definition belongs to the enemy. An army which lacks confidence is defeated before it takes the field. This is why God commanded Gideon to announce to the Israelites: "Whosoever is fearful and afraid, let him return and depart early from Mount Gilead" (Judges 7:3).

A THEOLOGY OF SHIPWRECK What we have seen, especially since the First World War, is a retreat from victory by Christians. Precisely at the time when humanism's hopes of a perfectible earth were shattered on the battlefields of Europe, the Christians also gave up hope. The Christians had seen the technological victories of secularism, and they had mentally equated these victories with Christ's kingdom promises. When the secular ship went down in a sea of needlessly shed blood, the Christians grabbed the only life preservers they thought were available: pessimistic eschatologies. They took comfort from the fact that the ship had sunk, not because they were safely sailing on a rival ship, but because *all* optimistic endeavors are supposedly doomed. They had built no ship of their own to compete with the *Titanic* of secularism, so they comforted themselves by clinging to theologies of universal sunken ships.

There are those who parade a theology of ship designing. They say that we ought to conquer the earth by means of Christian institutions. They claim that they have designs ready and waiting—cosmonomic designs, certified for export by the Dutch board of trade—but that they know, in advance, that there is no market for such designs, no capital to begin construction, and no hope of seeing them completed. They feel that they have been faithful to the Bible by merely proclaiming the hypothetical possibility of the external kingdom of God on earth. They have not bothered to get down to the blueprint stage, simply because they have not believed that their social and economic designs could ever be implemented. All ships, ultimately, are doomed, say these theologians of shipwreck.

Is it surprising, then, that the "dominies" in clerical robes are considered to be immune to criticism by laymen within ecclesiastical organizations that are based on a theology of shipwreck? After all, if all secular ships must go down eventually, and all Christian social institutions are equally doomed, then the only hope is the lifejacket of internal victory. *Spiritual victory* is all that counts, since this alone will float in a sea of social chaos. And, we must always remember, it is only ordained pastors who pass out the lifejackets. They have the keys to the kingdom, meaning the sacraments, preaching, and institutional discipline within the churches. This is the only kingdom there is, if not theoretically, then at least practically. The kingdom is finally equated with the institutional church and its operations, despite the fact that Protestant theologians officially reject this medieval vision of the kingdom. Where there is no victory possible, there we find no theology of dominion.

ESCHATOLOGY AND TYRANNY
If men have no hope of being able to reform the external world — the world outside the institutional churches — then they are faced with two sources of tyranny. The first is ecclesiastical. The second is political.

Ecclesiastical tyranny stems from the monopoly position which pastors are understood to enjoy within the confines of the institutional churches. If the internal kingdom is the only hiding place for weary, beaten laymen — inevitably defeated in a world devoid of Christ's power — then laymen must accept this resting place on the terms assigned to them by the ordained leadership. A monopoly can extract monopoly returns, after all. The only competition faced by the clerics, given an eschatology of external defeat, is that offered by other clerics in other churches. The world offers no comforts, no hope of successes enjoyed by faithful Christians, no promise of dominion in terms of biblical revelation. The only hope of victory is the victory of the life-jacket. Of course, other churches can offer life-jackets. This reduces the power of the defenders of Protestant sacerdotalism, but it does not eliminate it. Laymen, in relation to their ecclesiastical superiors, can only play off one against another; they cannot exercise comparable authority in any significant sphere of life officially belonging to them, because their spheres of legitimate authority are battlefields of guaranteed defeat. At best, laymen can be generals of rag-tag armies of incompetents.

An eschatology of shipwreck also leaves men virtually helpless against the unwarranted demands of an expanding civil government. Humanism may be bankrupt, but Christians—who own moral and cultural capital because of their relationship with Christ—are unwilling to make a "run on the banks" of humanism. Therefore, the State expands its naked power, since few voices are raised in *principled protest*. The Christians remain silent, or at least confused in their opposition, precisely because they have been taught that impotence politically and culturally is their assigned task on earth. There are two realms, spiritual and secular, and the secular realm is one of chaos and defeat. Why spend time in principled protest, if the only possible result is defeat? How much capital—energy, time, money, commitment—will men invest in a venture which has attached to it the theological equivalent of a Bad Housekeeping seal of approval?

CONCLUSION So what we find in the twentieth century is a twofold expansion of power, first by the defenders of Protestant sacerdotalism, and second by the secular State. The State needs pastors who preach a theology of defeat. It keeps the laymen quiet, in an era in which Christian laymen are the most significant potential threat to the unwarranted expansion of State power.

4

FUNDAMENTALISM: OLD AND NEW

> ". . . old fundamentalists are becoming new fundamentalists, and the . . . new fundamentalists are preaching a *vision of victory.*"

Historians always get themselves in trouble when they announce, "On this date, a new movement was born." Their colleagues ask them, if nothing else, "How long was the pregnancy, and who was the father?" The so-called "watersheds" of history always turn out to be leaky.

With this in mind, let me plunge ahead anyway. I contend that there is one event by which you can date the institutional separation of the old fundamentalism and the new. It took place in August of 1980 in the city of Dallas, Texas. It was the National Affairs Briefing Conference. At that meeting, the "New Christian Right" and the "New Political Right" political technicians came together publicly and announced a new era in political cooperation. The conference went on for two days and featured dozens of speakers. The list included Pat Robertson, Jerry Falwell, James Robison (during the more political-oriented phase of his ministry), and Tim LaHaye, representatives of the "New Christian Right." The "New Political Right" speakers included Howard Phillips and Paul Weyrich. They even had me give a speech, after I had clawed my way in. (Howard Phillips was able to get me included.)

They invited all three Presidential candidates — Ronald Reagan, Jimmy Carter, and third-party candidate John Anderson — but only Ronald Reagan accepted. This was significant. President Carter had featured his "born-again" faith prominently in the 1976 election, and millions of fundamentalists took him at his word. "Trust me," he said, and they did. By 1980, it was clear to everyone that Carter had not appointed any Christian to a position of influence anywhere in his cabinet. While President Reagan later imitated Carter by also ignoring the Christians and by relying on Trilateral Commission members and Council on Foreign Relations members to staff his cabinet (CFR Team-B, Susan Huck once called it), this was not generally expected in August of 1980. (I had expected it and said so in print before the election, but I am extremist.) By 1980, the old fundamentalists felt betrayed by Carter — for some reason, more than they now feel betrayed by Reagan — and they voted overwhelmingly for Reagan, whose theology was far less visible than Carter's had been.

The message of the conference was straightforward: it is the Christian's responsibility to vote, to vote in terms of biblical principle, and to get other Christians to vote. There can be no legal system that is not at bottom a system of morality, the speakers repeated again and again. Furthermore, every system of morality is at bottom a religion. It says "no" to some actions, while allowing others. It has a concept of right and wrong. Therefore, everyone concluded, it is proper for Christians to get active in politics. It is our legal right and our moral, meaning religious, duty.

You would think that this was conventional enough, but it is not conventional at all in the Christian world of the twentieth century. So thoroughly secularized has Christian thinking become, that the majority of Christians in the United States still appear to believe that there is neutrality in the universe, a kind of cultural and social "no man's land" between God and Satan, and that the various law structures of this neutral world of discourse are all acceptable to God. All except one, of course: Old Testament law. That is unthinkable, says the modern Christian. God will accept any legal framework except Old Testament law. Apparently He got sick of it 2000 years ago.

So when the crowd heard what the preachers and electronic media leaders were saying, they must have booed, or groaned, or walked out, right? After all, here were these men, abandoning the political and intellectual premises of three generations of Protestant pietism, right before the eyes of the faithful. So what did they do? They clapped. They shouted "Amen!" They stood up and cheered.

These men are master orators. They can move a crowd of faithful laymen. They can even move a crowd of preachers. Was it simply technique that drew the responses of the faithful? Didn't the listeners understand what was being said? The magnitude of the response, after two days of speeches, indicates that the listeners liked what they were hearing. The crowds kept getting larger. The cheering kept getting louder. The attendees kept loading their packets with activist materials. What was going on?

VICTORY They were, for the first time in their lives, smelling political blood. For people who have smelled nothing except political droppings all their lives, it was an exhilarating scent. Maybe some of them thought they smelled something sweet back in 1976, but now they were smelling blood, not the victory of a safe "born again" candidate like Jimmy Carter once convinced Christians that he was. They were smelling a "throw the SOB's out" victory, and they loved it. Only Reagan showed up. Carter and Anderson decided the fundamentalists wouldn't be too receptive to them. How correct they were.

But it was not simply politics that motivated the listeners. It was everything. Here were the nation's fundamentalist religious leaders, with the conspicuous exception of the fading Billy Graham, telling the crowd that the election of 1980 was only the beginning, that the principles of the Bible can

become the law of the land, that the secular humanists who have dominated American political life for a
hundred years can be tossed out and replaced with
God-fearing men. Every area of life is open to Christian victory: education, family, economics, politics,
law enforcement, and so forth. Speaker after speaker
announced this goal to the audience. The audience
went wild.

Here was a startling sight to see: thousands of
Christians, including pastors, who had believed all
their lives in the imminent return of Christ, the rise
of Satan's forces, and the inevitable failure of the
church to convert the world, now standing up to
cheer other pastors, who also had believed this doctrine of earthly defeat all their lives, but who were
proclaiming victory, in time and on earth. Never
have I personally witnessed such enthusiastic schizophrenia in my life. Thousands of people were cheering for all they were worth—cheering away the
eschatological doctrines of a lifetime, cheering away
the theological pessimism of a lifetime.

Did they understand what they were doing? How
can anyone be sure? But this much was clear: the
term "rapture" was not prominent at the National
Affairs Briefing Conference of 1980. Almost nobody
was talking about the imminent return of Christ.
The one glaring exception was Bailey Smith, President of the Southern Baptist Convention, who later
told reporters that he really was not favorable to the
political thrust of the meeting, and that he came to
speak only because some of his friends in the evangelical movement asked him. (It was Smith, by the

way, who made the oft-quoted statement that "God doesn't hear the prayer of a Jew." Ironically, the Moral Majority got tarred with that statement by the secular press, yet the man who made it had publicly disassociated himself from the Moral Majority. He has since disavowed the statement, but he certainly said it with enthusiasm at the time. I was seated on the podium behind him when he said it. It is not the kind of statement that a wise man makes without a lot of theological qualification and explanation.)

In checking with someone who had attended a similar conference in California a few weeks previously, I was told that the same neglect of the rapture doctrine had been noticeable. All of a sudden, the word had dropped out of the vocabulary of politically oriented fundamentalist leaders. Perhaps they still use it in their pulpits back home, but on the activist circuit, you seldom hear the term. More people are talking about the sovereignty of God than about the rapture. This is extremely significant.

MOTIVATION   How can you motivate people to get out and work for a political cause if you also tell them that they cannot be successful in their efforts? How can you expect to win if you don't expect to win? How can you get men elected if you tell the voters that their votes cannot possibly reverse society's downward drift into Satan's kingdom? What successful political movement was ever based on expectations of inevitable external defeat?

The New Christian Right is feeling its political strength. These people smell the blood of the political opposition. Who is going to stand up and tell these people the following? "Ladies and Gentlemen, all this talk about overcoming the political, moral, economic, and social evils of our nation is sheer nonsense. The Bible tells us that everything will get steadily worse, until Christ comes to rapture His church out of this miserable world. Nothing we can do will turn this world around. All your enthusiasm is wasted. All your efforts are in vain. All the money and time you devote to this earthly cause will go down the drain. You can't use biblical principles — a code term for biblical Old Testament law — to reconstruct society. Biblical law is not for the church age. Victory is not for the church age. However, get out there and work like crazy. It's your moral duty." Not a very inspiring speech, is it? Not the stuff of political victories, you say. How correct you are!

Ever try to get your listeners to send you money to battle the forces of social evil by using some variation of this sermon? The Moral Majority fundamentalists smelled the opposition's blood after 1978, and the savory odor has overwhelmed their official theology. So they have stopped talking about the rapture.

But this schizophrenia cannot go on forever. In off-years, in between elections, the enthusiasm may wane. Or the "Christian" political leaders may appoint the same tired faces to the positions of high authority. (I use the word "may" facetiously; the Pied Pipers of politics appoint nobody except secular humanists. Always. It will take a real social and political upheaval to reverse this law of political life. That upheaval is coming.) In any case, the folks in the pews will be tempted to stop sending money to anyone who raises false hopes before them. So the "new" fundamentalist preachers are in a jam. If they preach victory, the old-line pessimists will stop sending in checks. And if they start preaching the old-line dispensational, premillennial, earthly defeatism, their recently motivated audiences may abandon them in order to follow more consistent, more optimistic, more success-oriented pastors.

What's a fellow to do? Answer: give different speeches to different groups. For a while, this tactic may work. But for how long?

THEOLOGICAL SCHIZOPHRENIA Eventually, the logic of a man's theology begins to affect his actions and his long-term commitments. We will see some important shifts in theology in the 1980's. We will find out whether fundamentalists are committed to premillennial dispensationalism — pretribulation, midtribulation, or posttribulation — or whether they are committed to the idea of Christian reconstruction. They will begin to divide into separate camps. Some will cling to the traditonal Scofieldism. They will enter the political arenas only when they are able to suppress or ignore the implications of their faith. Men are unlikely to remain in the front lines of the political battle when they themselves believe that the long-term earthly effects of their sacrifice will come to nothing except visible failure. Others will scrap their dispensational eschatology completely and turn to a perspective which offers them hope, in time and on earth. They will be driven by the implications of their religious commitment to the struggles of our day to abandon their traditional premillennialism. Pessimistic pietism and optimistic reconstructionism don't mix.

This is not to say that consistent premillennialists cannot ever become committed to a long-term political fight. It is to say that *most* premillennialists have not done so in the past, and are unlikely to do so in the future. If they do, leadership will come from other sources, theologically speaking.

Three basic ideas are crucial for the success of any religious, social, intellectual, and political movement. First, the doctrine of *predestination*. Second, the doctrine of *law*. Third, the doctrine of *inevitable victory*. The fusion of these three ideas has led to the victories of Marxism since 1848. The Communists believe that historical forces are on their side, that Marxism-Leninism provides them with access to the laws of historical change, and that their movement must succeed. Islam has a similar faith. In the early modern Christian West, Calvinists and Puritans had such faith. Social or religious philosophies which lack any one of these elements are seldom able to compete with a system which possesses all three. To a great extent, the cultural successes of modern secular science have been based on a fusion of these three elements: scientific (material) determinism, the scientist's knowledge of natural laws, and the inevitable progress of scientific technique. As faith in all three has waned, the religious lure of science has also faded, especially since about 1965, when the counter-culture began to challenge all three assumptions.

Without a doctrine of the comprehensive sovereignty of God, without a doctrine of a unique biblical law structure which can reconstruct the institutions of society, and without a doctrine of eschatological victory, in time and on earth, the old fundamentalists were unable to exercise effective political leadership.

The prospects for effective political action have begun to shake the operational faith of modern fundamentalists — not their official faith, but their operational world-and-life view. This shift of faith will steadily pressure them to rethink their traditional theological beliefs. The leaders of the moral majority movement will come under increasing pressure, both internal and external, to come to grips with the conflicts between their official theology and their operational theology.

It is doubtful that many of the leaders will announce an overnight conversion to the long-dreaded optimistic faith. It is doubtful that they will spell out the nature of the recently rethought world-and-life view. But younger men will begin to become more consistent with their own theological presuppositions, and those who adopt the three crucial perspectives — predestination, biblical law, and eschatological optimism — will begin to dominate the moral majority movement. It will take time, and older, less consistent leaders will probably have to die off first, but the change in perspective is predictable. The taste of victory will be too hard to forget.

CONCLUSION After more than half a century of political hibernation, fundamentalists began to get actively involved in national politics in the election of 1980. Many of the leaders of the older, pietistic, "don't get involved in worldly affairs" version of American fundamentalism made a major switch in their ministries between 1976 and 1980. Jerry Falwell is the most prominent example, but he was not alone. There were several reasons for this: opposition to abortion, opposition to humanism in public education, opposition to moral decay, opposition to Carter's submissive foreign policy, opposition to the visible deterioration of our national defense system. But most important was a new outlook concerning the possibility of external victory — victory prior to the visible, personal return of Jesus Christ to earth. What has been most remarkable (and utterly ignored by the secular and Christian press) is this *shift in practical eschatology*. Slowly, and not all that surely, old fundamentalists are becoming new fundamentalists, and the "litmus test" of this shift in perspective is the issue of eschatology. The new fundamentalists are preaching a *vision of victory*.

5

WHY FIGHT TO LOSE?

"It is time for Christians to stop giving Satan credit for more than he is worth. Christians must stop worrying about Satan's power, and start working to undermine his kingdom."

"There is no substitute for victory."

Gen. Douglas MacArthur

Most people want to know how to invest their money. What would you think about the following investment? I have found a brand new company that needs financing. It is operated by inexperienced managers who have never been in management positions before. It has a very small budget. It has no government grants of any kind; in fact, the government has already convicted the president of the company for making fraudulent claims. There are no college graduates employed by the company. All the major institutions of higher learning teach a totally different management program and refuse to recognize this firm's techniques as valid.

So far, it doesn't sound too promising. But let me add a few more observations. The firm's product line has been deliberately designed to be out of fashion with the buying public's tastes. It has no advertising budget. The recently recruited sales force is expected to do door-to-door marketing, and they have had no experience in this field. The only experience in direct marketing that the managers had was regional, over the last three years, and the firm suffered tremendous sales resistance in this market. Nevertheless, the firm is determined to go international.

Would you invest in this company? More to the point, would you put everything you own into the company?

But I forgot to tell you something. The firm's president is no longer being held by the government. He is now in conference with the chief executive officer, who happens to be his father, and who is the developer of the most brilliant sales and recruiting package the world has ever seen. Not only that, the developer of the program has made sales projection figures that are comprehensive, and which in the past have always proven accurate. He says that the company will eventually dominate the world market.

Now would you invest in the company? Maybe, *if* you believed in the developer and his son.

A little less than 2,000 years ago, a handful of Jews in Palestine were given just this opportunity. They took advantage of it. Of the original twelve "senior managers," one defected to the "rival firm," but died shortly thereafter. He was replaced. Within two months, thousands of recruits from all over the world were brought into the sales force. They returned home with reports on what they had been told. The firm started growing faster than its rivals had believed possible.

The organization is still "in business" today. It's called the church of Jesus Christ.

HISTORICAL CONDITIONS IN THE FIRST CENTURY

When we think about the earthly odds against the early church, we can only marvel at what they accomplished. The Jews were against them. The Roman authorities were against them. The various rival Eastern cults, which were spreading like wildfire throughout the Empire, were against them. The church attracted its converts from the less prestigious groups in society. They had poor educations generally. Most of the early leaders were probably illiterate. How could they have hoped to succeed?

They had God on their side, of course. But God does not place His people into historical vacuums. He had created a unique set of conditions for them to work with. First, the Roman Empire had established an excellent communications and transportation system. The Roman highways were marvels of engineering. The Roman army kept them generally free of bandits, and the navy kept the Mediterranean free of pirates. Trade flourished.

With trade flourishing, people had to communicate. Two languages were universal: Greek and Latin. Both were advanced languages with literature;

they were both written languages, and an historically high percentage of literate people—far higher than four centuries before or later—were available to write and receive messages.

Second, people's faith in Greek and Roman religions was fading. There were dozens of Eastern cults coming into Rome. Magic, astrology, and fortune telling were on the rise, and the Roman government could not stamp them out. Religious anarchy was becoming a way of life.

Third, people had lost confidence in representative civil government. Alexander the Great destroyed the Greek democracies before he died in 322 B.C. His successors were declared gods. Augustus Caesar accepted deification by the provinces a few decades before Christ was born. His successors made his divinity official. What elected representative of the Roman people could claim to possess the power of a god?

Augustus downgraded the Roman Senate. Bloodshed soon ruled politics. The emperor Caligula came to the throne in 37 A.D. when his closest companion smothered the emperor Tiberius and then saluted his friend as emperor. Caligula, a madman, declared himself a god. Four years leter, two officers of the guard murdered him. The Senate tried to regain power one last time, but failed. The army installed Claudius, a fool. Fourteen years later, his fourth wife poisoned him. Her son, Nero, the last of the heirs of Augustus, came to power in 54 A.D. His teacher, the philosopher Seneca, had taught him that he was to become the savior of the world. He became a murderous tyrant. He even had his mother and his wife murdered. Who could trust in politics?

Fourth, the economy began to disintegrate. The emperors announced their divinity and the coming salvation of the world on the Roman coins. Steadily, they also debased the coinage. They removed the silver and substituted cheaper copper. Prices skyrocketed. Inflation began to erode people's faith in the economy.

Fifth, government welfare programs began to drain the Roman treasury. Free bread and circuses made high taxation mandatory. People stayed on the dole for so long that the right to receive government handouts became a hereditary right.

Sixth, sexual debauchery became common. The high ideals of the Roman family became little more than a memory. The upper classes no longer served as models for the rest of the citizenry. Pornography spread throughout the culture. Some of the walls of Pompei today are covered with pornographic paintings, as they were when the volcano erupted in 79 A.D. Some of Pompei's statuary is so foul that modern, "liberated" tourists are not even allowed to view it.

Seventh, the population of the upper classes stagnated. They practiced abortion and infanticide. They left their infants in the streets to die.

In short, the whole culture was disintegrating. When people lose faith in their institutions, they are ripe for a takeover by those who have a living faith.

THE CHURCH'S OPPORTUNITY The early church took advantage of this unique opportunity. They set up church courts to handle disputes, as Paul had commanded (I Corinthians 6). Their people received justice.

They built strong families. They went out and picked up babies who had been left to die. The authorities were outraged. This was made illegal. So the Christians violated the law. They kept taking home exposed infants.

They took care of their own people. They used the tithe to support the poor and sick among them. They did not go permanently on the dole.

They worked hard. They became the most productive citizens in the Empire. Yet they were persecuted. They refused to honor the "genius" (divinity) of the emperor. This was considered treason by the Roman authorities. Nero used tar-covered Christians as torches at his parties.

For over two centuries the church was persecuted. The persecution was intermittent. One generation would suffer, many would renounce the faith, others would compromise. The church would be "thinned out." Then, strengthened by resistance to persecution, the church would experience growth during periods of relative toleration.

Finally, the emperor Diocletian came to the throne, in 284. Inflation was rampant. He put on price and wage controls. Shortages immediately appeared. He imposed the death penalty for violators. The economy began to collapse. He persecuted the church. In 305, he gave up and abdicated—the first emperor ever to do so.

In 312, Constantine came to the throne. He

declared Christianity as the lawful religion. The first Christian emperor of Rome had arrived. The persecutions ended. Christians were brought into the civil government. Constantine recognized the obvious: there was no other social force in Rome stable enough, honest enough, and productive enough to match the Christian church. The Empire could no longer do without these people. After almost 300 years, *Christ had conquered Caesar.* The power of Rome had crumbled before the kingdom of God. God, through the faithfulness of His people, had vanquished His enemies.

CHRISTIAN SELF-GOVERNMENT The church had suffered. It had been reviled, ridiculed, beaten down. But over the years, Christians learned how to deal with adversity. They had learned to deal with reality. There was no Roman State to rely on for justice or protection. They had to rely on God, on themselves, and their church courts. *They became a second government within the Empire.* When the time was ripe, they were ready to exercise leadership.

But what about today? Are Christians ready to exercise leadership in the high places of our world? Where are the Christians? Almost invisible.

Why? Why are people who believe in the God of Abraham, Moses, David, Elijah, and Christ almost invisible in today's culture? We live in a culture built by Christians, from the days of Constantine to the days of America's Founding Fathers, almost all of whom were members in good standing in Bible-believing churches. But we have very little say in today's world.

Where can we point to and say, "There's where we're dominant"? In the universities? Hardly; they are all controlled by people who believe that the God of the Bible is irrelevant in the classroom, except to be ridiculed.

In civil government? Where are the Bible-based laws? Where are men able to get elected by campaigning as Bible-believing, Bible-following students of righteousness?

What about entertainment? Debauchery at worst, stupidity at best. The Christians have virtually no influence in this area.

The media? Not on the major networks. Not in the important newspapers. No magazine with national impact acknowledges Christ as king.

In the courts? Where abortion has been legalized? Where a man who shoots the President can be acquitted by reason of insanity? What is really crazy is the law.

We have to face it: *there is hardly a single area where Christians have distinguished themselves as the best in the field*. In Bible translating, yes. In running foreign orphanages, yes. But not in the corridors of power or influence.

"THE BIBLE HAS THE ANSWERS!" That's what we tell people. We go to them with the Word of God, and we tell them that they can find the solutions to the problems that are destroying them. But do we believe it? Do we *really* believe it?

What if he is a Senator who faces defeat if he votes

for (or against) a particular bill. Does the Bible tell
him which way to vote? What if he is a businessman
who is considering borrowing money for a project.
Does the Bible give him instruction?

What if he is a judge who is about to sentence a
criminal? Does the Bible give him guidelines?

Humanists are convinced that the Bible should
not be used as a blueprint for society. As a matter of
fact, the vast majority of seminary professors, even
in Bible-believing seminaries, agree with the humanists on this point. But if they are correct, then
*what can we use to guide us in our search for right and
wrong*? Our own imaginations? What we learn in
university classrooms taught by humanists? What
we read on the editorial page of the *New York Times*?

If not in the Bible, then where?

This is the question Christians have been avoiding
for a century.

A "KING'S X" FROM GOD? Christians take the
message of salvation to lost men. Why? To tell them
about the penalties of sin, and God's grace in providing an escape from judgment, through faith in
Jesus Christ. Without a knowledge of sin, Paul
wrote to the church at Rome, there can be no knowledge of the new life in Christ (Romans 7:9-12).

Then what do we tell men who are sinning in high places?
The prophets of Israel told kings right to their faces
what they had done, and what God was going to do
to them if they failed to repent. They were very
specific in their charges against the rulers of the day.

But if men can sin in high places, they must be *sin-*

ning against something. They must be sinning against God's law. They must be defying God by disobeying His standards.

In short, *if there are no God-given standards of righteousness in every area of life, then there can be no call to repentance in every area of life.* But if we say this, then we are saying that sinful men can continue to do anything they want in these areas of life. We are saying that God gives to men a huge "King's X" in life.

There is no zone of neutrality, no "King's X" from God's standards of righteousness, anywhere in the universe. This is what we have to preach to men if they are to be saved from their sins.

GOD'S COMPREHENSIVE JUDGMENT Sinful man wants to believe that he can escape the judgment of God. He wants to believe that he is free to do whatever he pleases, from morning to night. He does not want to hear the voice of God.

Modern Christian preaching tends to give sinful man what he wants. It tells him that he is "a little" off the mark. He is "not quite" righteous before God. There are "certain areas" of his life that are not being lived in terms of God's requirements. But on the whole, sinful man is really not all that sinful. So he is told.

The prophets of Israel pulled no punches. They went to kings and commoners, priests and rich men, and told them that they were corrupt, from top to bottom. They told them what they had done to violate God's law in every area of life: economics, agriculture, civil government, military strategy, foreign policy, religious worship, and family relations.

The prophets also reminded them of the warnings in Deuteronomy 28. There would be judgments from God: in economics, agriculture, civil government, military strategy, foreign policy, religious worship, and family relations. There is no escape. Sinners must repent.

In other words, *the Old Testament prophets closed the escape hatches*. They would not let the sinners off God's hook in any area of life. They told them that *God's judgment is comprehensive because men's sins are comprehensive*.

But we must never forget what kind of judgment the prophets preached: *judgment unto restoration*. God had them preach judgment unto destruction to the pagan nations around Israel (except for Jonah, when he preached in Nineveh). What we, too, must preach, is judgment unto restoration.

GOD'S COMPREHENSIVE SALVATION Every time the prophets warned the people about God's wrath, they told them why it was coming. They told the people to repent, meaning "to turn around." They told them to turn around from *specific sins* that were going to result in *specific judgments*.

But they also told them something else: *God will bring comprehensive restoration after His comprehensive judgments*. Isaiah said: "I will restore thy judges as at the first, and thy counsellors as at the beginning; afterward thou shalt be called, The city of righteousness, the faithful city. Zion shall be redeemed with judgment, and her converts with righteousness" (Isaiah 1:26-27).

He proclaimed to them the coming of "the acceptable year of the Lord" (Isaiah 61:2), in which the people of God "shall build the old wastes, they shall raise up the former desolations, and they shall repair the waste cities, the desolations of many generations" (Isaiah 61:4).

You have sinned, the prophets told them, and you shall be judged. *But God shall restore you*, even as you rebelled against Him, and even as He judged you: *comprehensively*. From head to toe, you shall be healed. From top to bottom, your entire culture shall be restored.

Restored to what condition? As it was in the beginning. What beginning? As it was when God delivered His law to Moses at Sinai, after the great deliverance of Israel out of Egypt. In short, Israel was to be *restored in terms of God's comprehensive law*, which they had rebelled against comprehensively.

Do modern Christians really believe this? Not many seem to. They do not confront the whole society with the call of repentance. They do not seem to recognize that our whole civilization is in rebellion against God, from top to bottom. They preach as though they think that the definition of sinning can be limited to a few things, such as adultery, or alcoholism, or heroin addiction, or nudity in the movies, or bad language on prime-time television, or prohibiting prayers in the public schools.

When a whole civilization is in rebellion, the whole culture is involved, every aspect of that culture. But you would not guess this from listening to today's sermons, even in supposedly conservative churches.

THE DOMINION ASSIGNMENT   God said to Adam and Eve: "Be fruitful, and multiply, and replenish the earth, and subdue it: and have dominion over the fish of the sea, and over the fowl of the air, and over every living thing that moveth upon the earth" (Gen. 1:28).

God said to Noah and his sons: "Be fruitful, and multiply, and replenish the earth" (Gen. 9:1).

God said to Abraham: "And I will make my covenant between me and thee, and will multiply thee exceedingly" (Gen. 17:2).

God said to Moses and the people of Israel: "The Lord shall make thee plenteous in goods, in the fruit of thy body, and in the fruit of thy cattle, and in the fruit of thy ground, in the land which the Lord sware unto thy fathers to give thee. The Lord shall open unto thee his good treasure, the heaven to give the rain unto thy land in his season, and to bless all the work of thine hand: and thou shalt lend unto many nations, and thou shalt not borrow. And the Lord shall make thee the head, and not the tail; and thou shalt be above only, and thou shalt not be beneath; if that thou hearken unto the commandments of the Lord thy God, which I command thee this day, to observe and to do them" (Deut. 28:11-13).

God said through the resurrected Christ: "All power is given unto me in heaven and in earth. Go ye therefore, and teach all nations, baptizing them in the name of the Father, and of the Son, and of the

Holy Ghost: Teaching them to observe all things whatsoever I have commanded you" (Matt. 28:18-20).

God said through the Apostle Paul: "Then cometh the end, when he shall have delivered up the kingdom to God, even the Father; when he shall have put down all rule and all authority and power. For he must reign, till he hath put all enemies under his feet" (I Cor. 15:24-25).

God said . . . but modern Christians prefer not to listen. They do not want to hear about their *comprehensive responsibility* to master the word of God, and to apply His standards in every area of life, bringing the whole world under the reign of Jesus Christ. They prefer to minimize their responsibility, calling men *out of the world*, rather than calling them to *rule over the world under the authority of Jesus Christ.*

SATAN'S COLLAPSING SOCIETY

We think that we are too weak, too unorganized, to achieve victory in social, political, and economic affairs. But look around us. What does the enemy have?

He has inflation one year and recession the next. In some years he has both at once. He has a culture filled with people who have lost faith in everything: God, law, the political system, the sanctity of marriage, and even physical survival.

Men without faith have difficulty in building anything permanent. People today have begun to lose faith in the future. Two generations ago, Americans were optimistic about the future. Today, they are glumly reconciled to seeing the loss of

American power, American honor, and the American dollar. *Men without hope are ripe for defeat by men who have hope.*

People are aborting their children, perhaps the ultimate rejection of the future. Their public, tax-supported schools are producing illiterate graduates by the millions every year. Welfare costs are exploding. The budgets of every nation are running huge deficits. No one knows where the money (with purchasing power) will come from to pay off Social Security obligations.

Our national defense system has fallen behind our enemy's. Our law enforcement organizations are virtually admitting defeat in the fight against crime.

In short, the society of Satan once again resembles the Roman Empire. It always must. We must not forget what happened to the Roman Empire. *Rome fell to Jesus Christ.*

A BIBLICAL WORLD-AND-LIFE VIEW The Bible speaks to every area of life. God holds men responsible for sinning in every area of life. God's law provides standards of righteousness in every area of life. The goal, then, is to learn what God requires of us, as individuals and as a society, and then humbly to begin to apply what we have learned.

We know that men cannot sin from morning to night and escape God's judgment. They must be called back to righteousness. In every area of life, they must first repent, and then return to their jobs as redeemed men, *to rebuild in terms of God's standards.* They must repair the damage their sinfulness caused.

They must make restitution.

In every area of life, we must reconstruct: in education, in medicine, in agriculture, in economics, in our occupations, in politics, in law enforcement, in family relationships, in church life, in the arts and sciences . . . in *everything*.

God has told us what we must accomplish, as individuals and as a nation, in order to fulfill our dominion assignment. There is no escape from this assignment, from Adam's day to the present. There can be personal success or failure in carrying it out, but no escape. God holds us responsible, as individuals and as a society. We have our marching orders from a God who has promised victory to His people, in time and on earth. *Victory can be achieved only in terms of God's righteousness, God's sacrifice at Calvary, and God's standards of righteousness for every realm of life.*

Satan cannot win. Why not? Because he has denied God's sovereignty and disobeyed God's law. But Moses was told explicitly, God's blessings come only from obedience. *Satan will not win because he has abandoned God's tool of dominion, biblical law.*

It is time for Christians to stop giving Satan credit for more than he is worth. Christians must stop worrying about Satan's power, and start working to undermine his kingdom. Contrary to a best-selling paperback book of the 1970's, Satan is not alive and well on planet earth—alive, yes, but not well. His troops are no better than their commander's strategy, and that strategy is flawed. They have been winning only because of the rival army's field-grade officers' failure to take their Commander's strategy seriously. When God-fearing officers finally begin to follow orders—the law of God—meaning that they begin to "do it by the Book," Satan's troops will be driven from the field.

6

1984, NOT 1948

"There is little likelihood that our perspective will be taken seriously until this culture works out its damnation without any fear or trembling."

What's wrong with our churches today? A lot. But if anything is wrong with the evangelical, officially conservative churches, it is this: the members think that the way to restore Christian culture is to return to 1948. At the very latest to 1956. That would be as close to "heaven on earth" as any church member could dare to hope for.

Because of the partial isolation of most of our churches from the grim reality of culture in the 1980's, they are reacting against the evils of 1968. They want to see a return of patriotism. They want dirty language off the prime-time T.V. shows. They want television starlets to put on some underwear. They dream of the day that Ozzie and Harriet will be the parent figures of America. (Trivia question: What did Ozzie do for a living?) The CBN commercial stations rerun "Father Knows Best" in the afternoon, or similar sitcom fare. Christian parents see these bland, thoughtless series as a kind of Novocain for their children's minds, or even their own minds. It takes them out of the 1980's.

In the Bible Belt the culture is still suffering from a mixture of three decades of rebellion. The 1950's style rebellion is almost cute: hot cars, cruising down main street, cigarettes behind the gym. These are the sorts of things that Fonzie does, and everyone loves Fonzie. The kid who was the black sheep in 1957, the kid your parents wouldn't have wanted you to goof off with, is a folk hero of the 1970's and 1980's — a throwback to "the good old days," when sin was essentially harmless. The trouble is, it was that "harmless" sin that served as a cultural wedge for the late 1960's. The same is true of the music. Buddy Holly was cute; the early Beatles were a bit strange looking, but cute. Nothing since 1965 has been cute.

Also present in the Bible Belt is the rebellion of the 1960's, such as pot smoking, illicit sex, loose language (I mean loose — incoherent — not just foul). Premarital sex, while frowned upon in Christian circles, is no longer a cause for mental breakdowns among parents. It is not exactly accepted, but it is not universally condemned, either. Incredibly, members of churches are not universally opposed to abortion. Thus, we come to the sins of the 1970's, such as having your daughter, "who made a mistake," kill her unborn child. In this case, the parents are as deeply involved in the sin as the children.

In the regions that see their rebellion on T.V., all nicely sanitized by the censors and the sponsors, Christian people can go about their business as if it were still 1962, as if our military defenses were still supreme, as if the Federal deficits were still in the $8 billion range, as if the public schools weren't in the process of academic collapse, as if their pensions were "as sound as a dollar," and the dollar were "as good as gold." They think they can insulate themselves from the economic crises of New York City and the moral crises of southern California. Their culture's walls still seem to be standing. If they can just get the local 7-11 store's manager to sell the soft-core pornography from a stack behind the counter, everything will be just fine.

The walls are in a state of disrepair. The universal culture of rock music, with its sado-masochistic lyrics, its call to homosexual experimentation, and all the rest of the filth, is available to any child able to reach up to the counter with $7.98, plus tax.

The public schools are the established churches of the religion of secular humanism, yet millions of Baptists in the South think of these schools as "our schools," and nothing short of a 2-and-10 football season can get them up in arms. If someone were to write a book on the South's approach to education, it might be called, *Pigskins, Sheepskins, and Lambs to the Slaughter*.

SHORTING OUT The cultural insulation of the Christian world has worn through all along the line.

When this happens to an electrical wire, it leads to power failures and fires. The same thing is true of cultures.

The evangelical world can no longer persist in the illusion that the American Republic is still operational as it was in the days of our Founding Fathers. It has gone the way of all flesh. The faithful are at ease in Zion. God has sent them fatness, and put leanness into their souls (Ps. 106:15).

The pastors of America are stuck. If they wish to model their ministries along the lines of the Old Testament prophets, all the fat, comfortable sleepers will stir, rub their ears, and grow angry. "Why are you preaching all this doom and gloom stuff? We get enough of that on T.V. We get that at the office all day long. We don't come to church to get more of the same. We come for relief." *They treat the church as if it were a giant glass of Alka Seltzer.* Relief is just a swallow away.

Want to shrink a ministry to the point of invisibility? Just start preaching specific sermons on specific sins that are dear to the hearts of the faithful. Just start teaching a view of Christian responsibility that goes beyond heart, hearth, and sanctuary. Recently, a relatively "concerned" evangelical church in Texas had the opportunity of bringing members out to hear some information on abortion and the possibility of setting up an abortion hot-line, to try to keep women from killing their children. Almost no members of this good-sized church showed up. "This sort of topic isn't spiritually uplifting," one member informed the pastor.

What is a pastor to do? *Preach the truth and clear the pews of slumberers.* But mortgages being what they are —churches are in debt, contrary to Romans 13:8— and pastoral employment opportunities being what they are, it is naive to expect this sort of preaching. In a typical church, the big-money donors have usually made their fortunes in terms of today's economic and political system. They do not want to rock the boat. They also want their pastor to refrain from rocking too hard.

But what if Deuteronomy is true? What if it applies? What if this nation is under a covenant, and the terms of breaking this covenant are those spelled out in Deuteronomy 28:15-68? What then? *Judgment.*

Now is the time for faithful Christians to start preaching for repentance, or judgment which leads to repentance. It appears that we are unlikely to wake up the slumbering faithful in the pews apart from judgment. So we should preach for judgment. Not judgment unto destruction, but *judgment unto restoration,* the kind of judgment preached by the prophets.

The culture is about to short out. God will not be mocked. We must be ready with lamps filled with oil, or to make the analogy more modern, generators filled with diesel, with 10,000 gallons buried safely nearby.

"DIESEL" One of the most important strategies of the Institute for Christian Economics is to make available books and newletters dealing with the specific sins of today's culture against God and His law. Not many people take these warnings seriously.

They did not take the prophets' warnings seriously, either. But when judgment came, and Zion ceased to be at ease, people then started examining their hearts and God's law to see what had happened to them. The I.C.E. is laying down a foundation of critical materials, as well as *construction materials*, so that after the signs of a crisis are obvious to the public at large, there will be a few thousand Christians who say to themselves first, and then to those around them, "I knew this was coming. I was warned. I was told of social, economic, and political alternatives. The law of God teaches that these sorts of crises are inevitable. If we want to reconstruct society, we need biblical alternatives to secular humanism. This time, we have to take God's word seriously."

We need diesel fuel for our generators. The publications of the I.C.E. serve as back-up supplies of diesel fuel. There is little likelihood that our perspective will be taken seriously until this culture works out its damnation without any fear or trembling. What these publications are designed to do is to sit on shelves in 3-holed notebooks, gathering dust. Most recipients probably ignore these materials today. We are investing long-term when we send them out. *We want people to wake up on the far side of some disaster, reach up to the dusty shelf, and start rereading our materials*. They will build then on foundations laid down today.

In a major crisis, every crackpot in the world will be parading in the streets (or the mails), telling anyone who will listen that "I told you this was coming! You had better listen to me." I will be among the crackpots, too, for I also warned you. But more important, I warned you because I took seriously the word of God, whereas the secular crackpots have ignored the explicit teachings of the Bible as thoroughly as the humanists in Washington have ignored them. That's what long-term social critics have to do: criticize. But to be effective in the long run, the critics must be *criticizing in terms of a framework*. They must be criticizing in terms of a reliable standard. That is what most other critics are not doing today.

So stock up on diesel. You may think you have no need of such information. But keep it around for a few years. It may surprise you in the future.

THE RUDE AWAKENING The rude awakening is coming. It always does. Men cannot go to sleep at the wheel indefinitely. There will be an accident. Or more accurately, there will be a nasty result. You cannot expect a civilization to sleep at the wheel forever, with the engine running at top speed, and not crash. Such crashes are hardly accidents.

When the awakening comes, there will be a frantic search for solutions—immediate, bread-and-butter solutions—and then scapegoats, and finally answers to existing problems. Woe to the man or movement that is discerned to be a scapegoat. What happened to the business community in the 1930's can happen to any group that is riding high in the days immediately preceding the crisis. What happened in Britain to the government of Neville Chamberlain in September of 1939 is only too typical.

Christians are not riding high today. It is not our

time yet. Others are riding high all over the world. They will ride no higher than the economy. They will ride no higher than their ability to "deliver the goods." Socialism, regulation, and inflation do not deliver the goods. They deliver only the "bads." The public will catch on only after a crisis, but the public *will* catch on.

This is why we need a remnant. We need a school of the prophets. We need men and women who know, in advance, that a crisis is coming. They also need to know why the crisis is coming, so that once it hits, they will be able with confidence to explain in retrospect why it came, and why certain concrete steps must be taken to see to it that such a crisis does not come again.

It is insufficient to stand on a streetcorner with a big sign that reads, "The End is Near." This familiar figure of the cartoonists is all around us: in every church that preaches the imminent return of Christ, in every humanist study group that teaches that nuclear war will end all life on earth, and in every government planning bureau that operates in terms of an economic philosophy which says that deflation will destroy civilization as we have known it. The end of the *humanists'* world may well be near. I believe it is. However, this is not the same thing as saying that the end of the world is near, unless we say that humanism is the highest and final stage of human history, or the worst and final stage of human history. Neither position is true. What we should say is that *humanism is Satan's most effective imitation of Christian culture*—a perverse mirror image—but that *it contains the seeds of its own destruction.* As it becomes more consistent with its own presuppositions, it will disintegrate.

We must be ready to pick up the pieces after the disintegration. We must be ready to show others how to do it. That is what the early church did for the collapsing Roman Empire. We must be ready to do it again.

7

CAPTURING THE ROBES

"The very same people who the fundamentalists regard as followers of Satan have set up the accreditation system, and the fundamentalist leaders have rushed to submit themselves to them in order to get their certificates of academic acceptability."

Robes are a symbol of authority in the West. The man who wears a robe as part of his profession has been invested with a degree of formal authority that other men do not possess. In the West, four groups wear robes: judges, university professors, ordained ministers, and church choirs. High school graduates and college graduates wear their robes once, and rent them. University professors are entitled to wear robes at special formal university affairs, and some (though probably very few) buy them. Only judges and ministers in the pulpit normally wear robes. Choirs also wear them, as agents of the church.

At the turn of the century, political and con-
spiratorial elites began a long-term program to "capture the robes" of American culture. They recognized the importance of judges, professors, and ministers. I remember hearing a speech by a former
Communist, Karl Prussion, in 1964, in which he told
of the assignment he received from the Party. He
became a theology student at Union Theological
Seminary in New York. The Party knew what it was
doing. The conservatives have not known what they
were doing.

LEFT-WING THEOLOGIANS *This World* is a new
scholarly journal, published by the American Enter-
prise Institute. Its perspective is that of the "neo-
conservative" movement, that is, men who are no
longer convinced concerning the wisdom of Federal
intervention into the economy, hostile to pacifism,
and conservative on social issues like abortion. The
Summer, 1982, issue presented the results of a remarkable opinion poll conducted by the Roper organization. It surveyed the political and economic
opinions of 1,112 seminary professors. Over half of
the 2,000 professors originally contacted responded
by giving answers to over 200 questions. The results
are worse than we might have imagined.

The professors, as a group, are self-consciously
left of center. As Ladd and Ferree summarized the
data, "Those who teach in schools of religion and
theology resemble fairly closely a larger community
of *academic humanists* of which they are a part" (p. 84).
On questions of marriage and abortion, they are

conservative, but not on politics and economics. Michael Novak writes: "Would you have guessed that, of all professors at all the Bible colleges, divinity schools, and seminaries in all fifty states, only 17 percent would call themselves Republicans (Q. 42)? Meanwhile, 62 percent call themselves either Democrats (30%) or independent, closer to Democrats (32%). Only 7 percent are pure independents. These figures help explain how 56 percent voted for McGovern over Nixon (34%), 66 percent for Carter over Ford (28%), and 52 percent for Carter over Reagan (30%) and Anderson (11%)" (p. 102).

"Eighty percent think the competition between the U.S. and U.S.S.R. is fundamentally a struggle in power politics, only 20 percent fundamentally a moral struggle (p. 103) . . . Seventy percent think U.S. multinational corporations hurt poor countries in the 'Third World,' 30 percent think they help (Q. 104). Thirty percent think the U.S. treats Third World countries fairly, 70 percent unfairly (Q. 105)" (p. 104).

Are these all theological liberals? While only 27 percent believe in the inerrancy of the Bible, 64 percent claim it is infallible in matters of faith and morals. Some 59 percent say they have had a born-again experience. Half claim they experience a special closeness to God daily (p. 105). These are people, in other words, who for the most part would be considered theological brothers by the editors of *Christianity Today, Eternity, Christian Life*, and virtually all of the non-denominational Christian magazines of America. Three quarters of these professors think the Moral

Majority is politically and religiously harmful (pp. 105-6).

Ladd and Ferree make an interesting comparison between prestige universities and liberalism, and between liberalism and the Ph.D.

> In various publications including *The Divided Academy* Ladd and Lipset demonstrated that within academe, confounding a "class theory of politics," the "top" is more liberal than the "bottom." When one arrays faculty, for example, by the intellectual standing of the college or university at which they teach, one finds that with every step up the institution-quality hierarchy there is a greater measure of faculty liberalism. Similarly, within any type of university or college, professors with greater academic attainments— measured, for example, in terms of levels of scholarly publication—are consistently more liberal than their less-attaining colleagues. . . .
>
> One sees reflections of this signal relationship in the political orientations of groups with the theological faculty. Those whose career emphasis has been nearest the academic and scholarly emphasis of the "main-stream" American professorial community appear consistently more liberal in sociopolitical outlook than those less involved in conventional academic work and attainment. For example, *theology faculty who hold the rank of Ph.D. are more liberal on every social and political issue measured in the survey* than are those with other academic

degree experience—persons with doctorates in religion, with masters and bachelors of divinity degrees, and so forth. This holds for the entire religion faculty as well as throughout the various denominational groups (p. 86.).

The obvious conclusion is simple: conservative fundamentalists who run the handful of colleges that fundamentalist students attend must cease requiring the Ph.D. from their faculty members. Indeed, anyone holding the Ph.D. in the humanities must be screened extra carefully to insure that he is not a liberal. What, in fact, are these colleges doing? "Upgrading" their faculties by requiring the Ph.D. The suicide of the evangelicals, institutionally, is assured. The liberals have convinced them that they must structure their colleges "the liberals' way." The academic inferiority complex of American evangelicals is used by the Left to capture their schools, from Biola College to Wheaton, from Westmont to Gordon-Conwell. Even the six-day creationist school, Christian Heritage College, sought and gained accreditation. Jerry Falwell hired a lawyer to force the accreditors to accredit his Liberty Baptist College. In short, *the fundamentalists simply will not learn.* They seek certification from those same elitist groups that they say are undermining Western civilization. *The very same people who the fundamentalists regard as followers of Satan have set up the accreditation system, and the fundamentalist leaders have rushed to submit themselves to them in order to get their certificates of academic acceptability.*

Who are the most liberal faculty members? Episcopalians, who were 78 percent liberal. Who were the most conservative? The Pentecostals, who were 75 percent conservative (p. 72). Regarding the question of "the biblical view of creation," 63 percent oppose the requirement that it be taught alongside of evolutionism in the public schools (Q. 22). (59 percent of the "other" group favored it—the tiny splinter groups, and independents, such as Pentecostals.) Regarding the requirement that the public schools set aside time daily for silent prayer, 68 percent oppose the idea (Q. 21).

An obvious conclusion is that the two favorite campaigns of the fundamentalist leadership—to get prayer back into the public schools and to get six-day creationism into their curricula—are doomed. Neither will find support from the theologians, and both will encounter overwhelming opposition from the humanists and liberal lawyers. It is unwise to devote any more energy or money to these two causes. This is what the fundamentalist leadership will not acknowledge. They would rather tilt at windmills than use the money to set up additional independent Christian schools, or to finance six-day creation curricula for the existing Christian schools.

ANTINOMIANISM AND LIBERALISM Another aspect of the survey which is important is its discovery of a fact that the Christian reconstructionists have pointed out for years, namely, that those who say that the Bible provides no blueprint for society's institutions tend to hold social views that are similar to those held by non-Christians in the community in general. *They simply "baptize" the prevailing opinions of their non-Christian peers.* In academic circles, this means the opinions of the intellectual elite.

To the question, "Do you think the Bible offers a blueprint for the ideal social system or not?", 77 percent said no. Two-thirds of the "others"—fundamentalist independents—agreed with the liberals on this point (Q. 24). *Do you see why the "others"—the intellectual leaders of the fundamentalist movement—are incapable of sustaining a successful challenge, theologically or institutionally, against the liberals?* Do you see why the liberals have captured Christian seminaries and colleges? Do you see why Ronald Sider's book, *Rich Christians in an Age of Hunger,* received no published criticism until David Chilton wrote *Productive Christians in an Age of Guilt-Manipulators?* Only because Chilton believes that biblical law is still binding on economics and politics could he refute Sider's "liberation theology." *The fundamentalists have been social antinomians. By rejecting God's law, they have necessarily accepted rule by the prevailing opinions of the day.* These opinions are humanistic. (For documentation of this assertion, see my essay, "The Intellectual Schizophrenia of the New Christian Right," in *Christianity and Civilization,* No. 1, published by the Geneva Divinity School, 708 Hamvasy, Tyler, Texas, 75701; $9.95).

CONCLUSION The battle for the mind, some fundamentalists believe, is between fundamentalism and the institutions of the Left. This conception of the battle is fundamentally incorrect. The battle for the mind is between the Christian reconstruction movement, which alone among Protestant groups takes seriously the law of God, and everyone else. There is no really serious "battle for the mind" between fundamentalists who accept accreditation and the liberals who control the accreditation mechanisms. The old-time fundamentalists, by accepting the liberals' view of social antinomianism — that the Bible offers no blueprint for social institutions, and therefore no program for Christian reconstruction — have become *epistemological humanists* in the realm of social theory. The older fundamentalists also adopted the *myth of neutrality* in educational theory and social theory. There is no "battle for the mind" here; only a loud debate between rivals for control of the accreditation committees and curricula development committees. And for three generations, the old fundamentalism has been losing the debate. It is a debate which should end with the fundamentalists walking out, leaving the liberals with no fundamentalist institutions to accredit. *Christians must stop fighting the battle for the mind by rules that the humanists have rigged in their favor.* (For a copy of *This World*, send $4 to them at 210 E. 86th St., New York, NY, 10028. Ask for the Summer, 1982, issue.)

[See the Glossary for definitions of Christian Reconstruction, fundamentalism, humanism, and law-order (the opposite of antinomianism).]

8

HUMANISM'S CHAPLAINS

". . . talk concerning a Christian world-and-life view is incredibly cheap; the test is this: What are the *sources and standards* for constructing a biblical alternative?"

The most important question of human knowledge is this one: "By what standard?" Is there some sort of universal logic which provides all mankind throughout all ages with a sufficient basis for making judgments? Or is the very idea of intellectual neutrality a snare and a delusion?

Historically, Christians and secularists have taken both sides. In their attempts to devise a universally valid intellectual defense of the faith, Christian apologists have appealed to "natural law" or "the law of non-contradiction," or some other common ground methodology. They have hoped that logic might bring rebellious men face to face with the claims of Christ. As Cornelius Van Til has demonstrated in numerous books, this appeal rests on the assumption of human autonomy, that is, the universally valid logic of human minds. It is an invalid presupposition. The only common ground is the sense of God's image in all men.

Secularists, especially prior to the mid-1960's, also appealed to "natural law" or "technocratic, non-ideological, pragmatic wisdom," in order to convince men of the universal validity of one or another program of social reconstruction. However, since the mid-1960's, this appeal increasingly has fallen on deaf ears; Marxists, revolutionaries of all brands, and systematic relativists have rejected the whole idea of a hypothetical universal logic. (Marx always rejected the idea.)

If there is no neutrality in human thought, then there is certainly no neutrality in any society's law structure. Laws are written to prohibit certain actions. These laws rest on the presupposition that certain acts are inherently wrong, according to a particular moral and religious order. There can be no law apart from a moral and religious law-order, and this law-order cannot possibly be neutral.

SOCIAL RECONSTRUCTION If men are to work out the implications of their religious faiths, then they will attempt to reconstruct the external institutions of society in terms of a particular law-order. Only a totally internalized religion can legitimately neglect the tasks of external renewal. Yet it is very difficult to imagine how such a totally internalized religion might operate. How can we speak of ethics

—human action within the framework of moral law—apart from external effects on other people and the creation? Even a pole-sitting ascetic is making a statement about his relationship with the world, and he has to have someone supply him with food, water, and clothing, not to mention volunteer "bedpan" services. He is absorbing the scarce economic resources of the creation in his attempt to demonstrate his supposed withdrawal from the affairs of mankind. He is making a statement about the proper way to live in this world, which implies a moral obligation on others either to imitate him or to acknowledge the legitimacy of his activities (inactivities).

This is why it is impossible, or at least extraordinarily difficult, to imagine an ethical system which has no vision of social reconstruction, no blueprint for society at large. Yet it is popular today within Christian circles to make grandiose pronouncements concerning the immorality of grandiose pronouncements regarding society. "No creed but the Bible, no law but love," we are told—a rigorous creed, to be sure—and from this presupposition, men have created systematic ethical systems justifying retreat. The pilgrim motif replaces the Christian soldier motif. The social irrelevance of modern Christianity is defended on principle, as if social irrelevance were an ethical goal to be pursued in a disciplined fashion.

Nevertheless, when we examine the calls for social neutrality, we find that in all known cases, the program of social neutrality winds up baptizing some humanistic program of social order. The Christian is told to make his peace with one or another non-Christian social order. The Christian is told to refrain from actively opposing, and then replacing, the prevailing social order.

Christians are *in* the world (a geographical identification), but not *of* the world (a spiritual identification). The question is: Should Christians attempt to subdue the world in an attempt to make it conform more closely to God's guidelines for external institutions? More to the point: *Are* there biblical guidelines for social institutions? If not, have we not asserted a fundamentally demonic universe, wherein neither we nor the devil may be judged for our actions, since we have violated no godly standards?

In short, isn't the argument for neutrality — neutrality in any sphere of human thought or life — an argument for autonomy? Isn't it an assertion of some universal "King's X," an ever-growing area of human action (or inaction), in which God may not legitimately bring judgment, precisely because He has no standards of action that apply? Isn't the idea of social neutrality a defense of the idea that man and Satan can live beyond good and evil?

RECONSTRUCTION Dr. Martyn Lloyd-Jones was one of the most respected preachers in England. His books have been published and widely read in the United States as well. He was trained as a physician, but he left medical practice to become a minister. He became an important advocate of Christian surrender to the world, and because of his prominence, we should examine his blueprint for "Christian inaction," or to be more precise, his blueprint for humanistic reformism.

Dr. Lloyd-Jones spelled out the details of his thinking in an essay, "The French Revolution and After," published in Britain in the book, *The Christian and the State in Revolutionary Times* (Westminster Conference, 1975). His essay makes the following points: 1) Christians must not support the status quo; 2) Christians must work for reform; 3) all explicitly Christian reforms will fail; 4) political conservatism is anti-Christian; 5) free market economics must be rejected. These same five points can be found in the exposition of seemingly endless proclamations made by respectable, educated, and frequently quoted Christian leaders, especially those in the neo-evangelical camp, the Toronto (neo-Dooyeweerdian) camp, and the "reprinting neo-Puritan" camp. This is the reigning ideology in the Grand Rapids-Toronto-Wheaton-Edinburgh-London-Amsterdam circuit.

Here is the message from Dr. Lloyd-Jones. He admits that we must have a total world-and-life perspective. "The Christian is not only to be concerned about personal salvation. It is his duty to have a complete view of life as taught in the Scriptures" (p. 101). This is a common theme of most educated Christian leaders: the need for a biblical perspective. It is this statement which is expected to serve as a sort of cleric's collar for "truly progressive" Christians—a means of distinguishing oneself from the old fundamentalism, whose advocates have not generally bothered themselves with questions of philosophy. Whether you're in Grand Rapids or Wheaton, London or Toronto, Christian academics will tell you of the need for a distinctly Christian perspective. This makes sense; the kicker is found in their *universal unwillingness to use revealed biblical law as the blueprint* for constructing a Christian alternative. This is absolutely crucial, since *without a specifically biblical blueprint, there is nothing left to choose except some humanist blueprint*. In short, talk concerning a Christian world-and-life view is incredibly cheap; the test is this: What are the *sources and standards* for constructing a biblical alternative?

Second, Dr. Lloyd-Jones was adamant in opposing three important errors: 1) the status quo; 2) explicitly Christian political reform; 3) other-worldliness (pp. 103-5). The only trouble is, he never says how you can avoid all three simultaneously. The worst evil is the status quo, since "historically it has been the greatest danger" (p. 102). He minces no words: "For some strange reason one of the greatest temptations to a man who becomes a Christian is to become respectable. When he becomes a Christian he also tends to make money; and if he makes money, he wants to keep that money, and resents the suggestion that he should share that money with others by means of taxation, etc. Looking at history it seems to me that one of the greatest dangers confronting the Christian is to become a political conservative, and an opponent of legitimate reform, and the legitimate rights of people" (p. 103).

Here we have it: the evils of political conservatism. He recognizes that there is a tendency for

Christians to make money. Sadly, he refuses to speculate concerning the reasons for this tendency to exist (and exist it does: Deut. 8, 28). But men who make money don't appreciate being forced by State bureaucrats to contribute money to the care and maintenance of statist power, i.e., welfare programs used for the purchase of votes by politicians, what Rushdoony has called the politics of guilt and pity. This, the good doctor argues, is an evil attitude on the part of Christians. They don't like to share their wealth with the State. The State, by implication, has a perfect right to the wealth of hard-working, thrifty, risk-taking Christians who have prospered financially. This is called "the legitimate rights of people." It is also called Keynesianism, interventionism, statism, the "new economics," political liberalism, the New Deal, the welfare State, the corporate State, and in the 1930's was known as fascism. It is theft with a ballot box instead of a gun. It is the Christian liberal's rewriting of the eighth commandment: "Thou shalt not steal, except by majority vote." It is the economics of most voters in Grand Rapids, Toronto, Wheaton, Edinburgh, London, and especially Amsterdam.

He recognizes that Anglo-Saxon Protestant Nonconformists—those opposed to an established State church—have traditionally been political reformists. These people were defenders of nineteenth-century political liberalism: political equality, but with economic freedom. He also recognizes that those defending the idea of the cultural mandate (Gen. 1:28) tend to be political reformers, as do the Marxist "liberation" theologians. In his interview in *Christianity*

Today (Feb. 8, 1980), he made clear his attitude toward the cultural mandate concept. Carl F. H. Henry asked him (from the perspective of neo-evangelicalism): "Would you agree that even if we might have only 24 hours or 48 hours, to withhold a witness in the political or any other arena is to withdraw prematurely from the social responsibility of the Christian and to distrust the providence of God? Might he not do something even in the last few hours that he had not done before? The closer we get to the end time, isn't it that much more important to address public conscience? Must we not press the claims of Christ in all the areas of society and remind people, whether they receive Christ or not, of the criteria by which the returning King will judge men and nations?" This is an excellent question, whether asked by a neo-evangelical, a neo-Dooyeweerdian, or a Christian reconstructionist. Dr. Lloyd-Jones' answer was quite explicit:

No; I'm afraid I don't agree. It seems to me that our Lord's own emphasis is quite different, even opposed to this. Take Luke 17 where we read, "As it was in the days of Noah, so shall it be also in the days of the Son of man. They did eat, they drank, they married wives . . . until the day that Noah entered into the ark, and the flood came. . . ." You can't reform the world. That's why I disagree entirely with the "social and cultural mandate" teaching and its appeal to Genesis 1:28. It seems to me to forget completely the Fall. You can't Christianize the world. The end time is going to be like the time of the Flood. The condition of the modern world proves that what we must preach more than ever is "Escape from the wrath to come!" The situation is critical. I believe the Christian people—but not the Church—should get involved in politics and in social affairs. The kingdom task of the church is to save men from the wrath to come by bringing them to Christ. This is what I believe and emphasize. The main function of politics, culture, and all these things is to restrain evil. They can never do an ultimately positive work. Surely the history of the world demonstrates that. You can never Christianize the world.

This tends to be the answer of the older fundamentalism: escape from the wrath to come, forget about Christian reconstruction. But what does he expect Christian people to do? Of course, it is not normally the task of the institutional church to get into the political arena. But that isn't the question. What about Christian men and women in voluntary political or other organizations? What can they expect to accomplish? Hardly anything, says the good doctor. They are in a losing battle. As he wrote in his 1975 essay:

We are now back to the New Testament position; we are like New Testament Christians. The world can never be reformed. Never! That is absolutely certain. A Christian State is impossible. All the experiments have failed. They had to fail. They must fail. The Apocalypse alone can cure the world's ills. Man even at his best, even as a Christian, can never do so. You can never make people Christian by Acts of Parliament. You can never christianize society. It is folly to attempt to do so. I would even suggest that it is heresy to do so (p. 108).

Here is his constant theme: men are sinful; the world is fallen; therefore, perfection is impossible. As he told Carl Henry, the cultural mandate was given to Adam before the Fall; we live as in the days of Noah. What he conveniently neglects—and he could not conceivably be ignorant of the passage—is that God gave the same cultural mandate to Noah, after the Flood (Gen. 9:1-7). It should be obvious why Dr. Lloyd-Jones conveniently neglects this passage: *it spells the doom of his entire misinterpretation of the Bible.* We cannot escape the moral burden of the cultural mandate—what I have called the dominion covenant—just because of man's ethical rebellion. We are the sons of Noah.

Christian reconstruction is supposedly impossible. However, we can work as Christians for reform. He calls statist wealth-redistribution "legitimate reform." He then appeals to the tradition of Abraham Kuyper. I find his conclusions most illuminating, especially in regard to the similarities drawn by Lloyd-Jones between the political careers of the Netherlands' Kuyper and Britain's first radical Prime Minister, Lloyd-George:

Nevertheless, government and law and order

are essential because man is in sin; and the
Christian should be the best citizen in the country. But as all are sinful, reform is legitimate
and desirable. The Christian must act as a
citizen, and play his part in politics and other
matters in order to get the best possible conditions. But we must always remember that
politics is "the art of the possible"; and so the
Christian must remember as he begins that he
can only get the possible. Because he is a Christian he must work for the best possible and be
content with that which is less than fully Christian. That is what Abraham Kuyper seems to
me to have done. I have recently read the life of
Kuyper again and it is clear that his enactments as Prime Minister and head of the Government were almost identical with the
Radicalism of Lloyd-George. They were two
very different men in many ways but their
practical enactments were almost identical.
The chief respect in which they differed was in
their view of education (p. 108).

This is damning Kuyper with faint praise.
Kuyper wanted government subsidies to Christian
schools, while Lloyd-George wanted the destruction
of all private education. Both men were caught up in
the ideology of economic interventionism by the
State, and this tradition still dominates the Toronto-
Amsterdam-Grand Rapids Dutch tradition, as well
as the British Protestant tradition. Yet there is
almost nothing in the Old or New Testament to war-
rant such a view of the State, which is why these

Christian defenders of the welfare State are unable to appeal to a body of biblical doctrine which might support their position.

So, we are told, individual action in support of the welfare State is valid, but reform in the name of Christianity is by definition impossible and therefore invalid, since politics is the art of the possible. He makes himself perfectly clear: we have no hope.

> I now come to what, to me, in many ways is the most important matter of all. I suggest that this is the main conclusion at which the Conference should arrive. The Christian must never get excited about reform, or about political action. That raises for me a problem with respect to the men of the 17th century and other times. It is that they should have become so excited about these matters. I would argue that the Christian must of necessity have a profoundly pessimistic view of life in this world. Man is "in sin" and therefore you will never have a perfect society. The coming of Christ alone is going to produce that. The Christian not only does not get excited, he never pins his hopes to acts of parliament, or any reform or any improvement. He believes in improvement, but he never pins his hope in it, he never gets excited or over-enthusiastic; still less does he become fanatical or bigoted about these matters (p. 108).

We *must* be pessimistic. Why, he doesn't say; we just ought to be. Then, given this pessimism, we have to face a pessimistic reality. We can never expect perfection; therefore, reform is impossible. We can work for it, but we should never get excited about it. Here is a counsel of despair, the psychology of defeat. Here also is verbal tomfoolery. What if I were to use this same line of reasoning against the legitimacy of the institutional church? First, we know we can never see a perfect church prior to Christ's second coming. Second, we should not get enthusiastic about church reform. Third, a Christian never puts his faith in church courts (or synods, or whatever), since the church can never be perfect. By equating "Christianity" with "perfection," Lloyd-Jones thereby emasculates applied Christianity. He negates institutional reform in the name of anti-perfectionism. The same syllogism, if applied to the institutional church, would destroy the institutional church, just as surely as it destroys the idea of a Christian social order. The premise (pessimism) is wrong, the goal (earthly perfection) is not what we expect to achieve, and the means (biblical law) are ignored.

ESTABLISHMENT RELIGION What Lloyd-Jones wants is simple: *the triumph of irrelevance.* If he didn't want it, he wouldn't argue so vehemently for its inevitability, especially in the face of the biblical testimony favoring victory, in time and on earth — not perfection, but victory. (See David Chilton's *Paradise Restored*, published by Reconstruction Press, P.O. Box 7999, Tyler, TX 75711; $14.95.) I am reminded of C. S. Lewis' words: "In a sort of ghastly simplicity we remove the organ and demand the function. We made men without chests and expect of them virtue and enterprise. We castrate and bid the geldings be fruitful." (*The Abolition of Man* [New York: Macmillan, (1947) 1967], p. 35.)

What he calls for — and what the overwhelming majority of widely read, academically respectable Christians call for — is *the defense of the status quo of the late twentieth century.* The modern status quo, being Darwinian, or Marxist, or in some other way evolutionistic, is based on the idea of change, whether reformist or revolutionary. It wants more government, not less; more State welfare, not less; more coercively enforced economic equality, not less; more taxation of the productive, not less. The modern status quo is the status quo of constant change — government-enforced experimentation. This is the legacy of the French Revolution, which Lloyd-Jones is so worried about, yet he has adopted it, though without its original optimism. He wants an economy of tinkering bureaucrats, for that is what the welfare State invariably produces, and he wants a welfare State. Because the language of the modern status quo is the language of change, our modern academic, non-fundamentalist Christians can wrap themselves in the flag of progress and change, when that flag is, in fact, the flag of the status quo. They can ignore biblical reconstruction — indeed, they feel compelled to oppose biblical reconstruction — which would forever abolish the humanist welfare State, with its constant economic intervention. These men are defenders of the humanists' evolutionary State. *They are the chaplains of humanism's bureaucracy.* They are the transmission belt of Fabianism in the world of evangelical Christianity. *Their job is to keep the silent Christian majority forever silent*, or, where the majority is no longer Christian, to keep the Christian minority fearful, despondent, and impotent. They have done their job very well. *They have been supremely victorious in this century in promoting the psychology of perpetual Christian defeat.* Chaplains for the status quo, they have paraded in the uniforms of "impossibility thinking" — the impossibility of Christian reconstruction in today's society of humanistic evolutionism.

What Lloyd-Jones really resented was the free market. He shared this resentment with others in the Grand Rapids-Toronto-Wheaton-Edinburgh-London-Amsterdam Axis. He reserved his worst epithet for the free market: *Arminian*. "Arminianism over-stresses liberty. It produced the Laissez-faire view of economics, and it always introduces inequalties — some people becoming enormously wealthy, and others languishing in poverty and destitution" (p. 106). Get this: the free market *introduces* inequality. It apparently wasn't there before. This is not only poor logic, but it is inaccurate historically. As the voluminous researches of Prof. P. T. Bauer and other economists have demonstrated, the free market *reduces* economic inequality, and it also erodes the barriers — status quo, statist barriers — that tend to prevent upward and downward economic mobility.

What is so unique about Lloyd-Jones' resentment? Nothing. It is the standard, run-of-the-mill pap that has been stuffed into the heads of two generations of American college students, and three generations of British students. It is the same old Fabianism, the same old Keynesianism. It is the status quo. So, using the language of anti-status quo, Dr. Lloyd-Jones joined the ranks of the ordained chaplaincy of humanist conformity. He was a Conformist's conformist, and he was therefore granted the right to use the language of progressive reformism—so long as it was not promoted in the name of Christianity, so long as it abandoned any appeal to Old Testament law, and so long as it abandoned hope.

Is it any wonder that leadership like this has produced generations of socially impotent Christians? Is it any wonder that humanism, in the form of the welfare State, has triumphed? In the realm of society, the salt has lost its savor. We have been afflicted with chaplains who have actively promoted savorless salt. The sheep need better shepherds; they need shepherds who are not front men for political humanism's wolves.

9

HUMANISM'S ACCOMPLICES

"As far as most Christian campuses are concerned, the theology of retreat has accomplished the goals of the secularists: to snuff out the life-giving, society-reconstructing message of Christ to the whole of man's existence."

What general would attempt to lead his forces into battle without a specific battle plan? What military commander would be content with nothing more than verbal exhortations to his troops to "be victorious" or "win one for the folks back home"? Such noble exhortation, apart from a battle plan, equipment, and explicit instructions to subordinates, would be about as likely to produce victory as the endless repetition of "Have a nice day."

When we sing "Onward, Christian Soldiers," do we expect to lose on every battlefield? Do we expect constant defeat to be God's training ground for total victory? "Victory through defeat" may be the chosen strategy of those who organize American foreign policy, yet among the most vocal critics of America's foreign policy "experts" are concerned conservative fundamentalists who simultaneously hold a theological version of this same "victory through endless defeats" strategy. What is seen as a disaster for American foreign policy is promoted as the very heart of God's plan for the ages.

What we need, therefore, is a two-pronged program. First, we need a *strategy of victory*—a general plan, including confidence of ultimate success. Second, we need *concrete tactics*, including an integrated, well-understood program for every sphere of human life. In short, we need a positive eschatology and a developed program of biblical law. Confidence without distinctive and explicit programs is foolishness. But a distinctive program, apart from confidence in the competence of one's commander, is unlikely to defeat a dedicated, optimistic enemy who has his own integrated strategy of subversion.

AN EXCUSE FOR NO PROGRAM The various eschatologies of shipwreck in this century became popular when it became clear that Christians were offering no alternatives to the secular programs of a steadily sinking humanism. Since the politics of humanism was leading to visible disaster, it became imperative for Christians to devise a biblical set of alternative programs. Failing this, they were culturally doomed, since they would go down on secularism's sinking ship.

Secularism, however, had already eroded the epistemological foundations of Christian colleges, textbooks, and businesses. Christians had adopted the secular "climate of opinion" through a dead-end mixture of Christian revelation and secular philosophy. Men had long since decided to defend Christian truths by means of an appeal to secular logic. The famous apologetic approach of the professors at Princeton Theological Seminary is a classic example of this kind of intellectual syncretism. When Cornelius Van Til's Christian philosophical reconstruction smashed the intellectual foundations of the old Princeton apologetics, bringing men back to *sola scriptura* as the only valid principle for constructing an intellectual defense of the faith, twentieth-century Christians were presented with a great cultural burden. They can no longer escape their responsibility for the creation of a de-secularized program of Christian alternatives. They can no longer be content to sink with the ship of secularism. They must rebuild Christian culture.

This responsibility has nevertheless been ignored. While the recent Dutch Reformed conservative tradition has been willing to deny the validity of secularism in apologetics, it has also refused to present concrete, specific programs that are explicitly based on the categories of biblical law. Simultaneously, amillennial pessimism has eroded the hope of the Dutch in the possibility of comprehensive success for Christian institutions, in time and on earth. Thus, they have contented themselves with forming Christian schools (closely linked to Dutch churches),

Christian labor unions (which have no distinctly Christian economic approach to the analysis of wage rates), and Christian political parties (which are a political impossibility in twentieth-century America —another program of built-in failures). There is nothing wrong with these activities, but they are "holding actions"—the products of a "holding action" eschatology. They are not programs of victory, but *programs of cultural isolation*—testimonies to a fallen world which cannot respond to the presentation of a Christian witness.

American fundamentalism, to the extent that it has an approach to apologetics (philosophical defense of the faith), is mired deep in the old Roman Catholic-Princeton methodology of intellectual syncretism (mixture). Furthermore, American fundamentalists generally have adopted a premillennial, dispensational eschatology. Like amillennialism, premillennialism denies the possibility of cultural victory on earth prior to the physical, bodily return of Christ to set up a universal earthly kingdom. Again, it does little good, in the eyes of the consistent fundamentalist, to construct Christian cultural alternatives, except as a witness—a witness inevitably doomed to cultural failure.

Pessimism erodes the incentives to create detailed alternatives to collapsing secularism. Men can make a witness far more readily to Christ's offer of salvation of souls than they can to Christ's offered healing of human institutions. "Witnessing" for the fundamentalist means calling attention to the rot of secularism and then offering a *personal* life preserver to the listener. Fundamentalism offers a personal escape hatch to those trapped on secularism's sinking ship, and with so many trapped people, who has time to begin construction of another ship, especially when we know that all such construction projects are doomed in advance by premillennial timetables?

There is nothing that automatically prohibits fundamentalists from working in the "construction plants" of social theory, but a cost-benefit analysis based on premillennialism's shortened timetables will almost always come out negative: too much cost, not enough benefits. Tracts are cheaper and quicker to write and print than multiple treatises dealing with Christian social theory. You don't have to begin from scratch when you write a tract, or even a book critical of humanism's rot. You usually do have to begin from scratch when you start devising an explicitly Christian psychology, economics, politics, sociology, or whatever. There are a lot of "instant witnessing mixes" available to fundamentalists: just add holy water and stir. Baking from scratch is increasingly a lost art, not just in the kitchen, but also in the sanctuary, classroom, and boardroom.

PIETISM'S ECONOMICS In December of 1978, a midwestern company sponsored a seminar in Christian economics. It was a gracious but depressing attempt to assess the "state of the art" of Christian economics. Several of the one dozen attendees were theological liberals. Of the theological conservatives, only three had degrees in economics. There was agreement that the civil government is growing too powerful—the screening committee had seen to it that statists were not invited—but there was no agreement concerning a proper strategy of reconstruction. In fact, most of the participants thought that the battle had been lost a long time ago.

Two of the economists had Ph.D.'s. They both taught on state university campuses. The first one admitted that what he was teaching was not Christian economics. His assigned textbooks were traditional secular studies, including those that he wrote or co-authored. The only Christian aspects of his teaching, he said, were certain limited biblical examples of economic activities, such as Christ driving the moneychangers out of the temple because they were using a temple monopoly to extract higher than market prices from those who bought offerings inside the temple's gates. This is a solid analysis, biblically speaking, but it was not integrated into an overall Christian economics approach to the subject.

The second economist, a converted Unitarian, had been a Christian for about seven years, according to his testimony—and his presentation was a personal testimony, as he admitted, not a lecture on Christian economics. The man is a total pessimist, and almost certainly a dispensationalist. His message was all too typical. Bear in mind that there are not many Ph.D.'s in economics in the U.S. who have even a vague commitment to biblical revelation— probably under 75—and Christian colleges seldom can afford to hire them.

Here is his testimony, taken verbatim from the

tape of his talk. "I'm still confused, somewhat. . . . I have not been able yet to get it sorted out what it means to be an economist and also to be a Christian." Fair enough; then he should have stopped right there. But he didn't. He felt constrained to lay the foundations of defeat. "The world is not going to get better. It is under the domain of Satan. It was never under the domain of the Christian. It's under the domain of Satan. It's coming to an end, maybe quicker than we perceive. I wish to God it were today. So out of this chaos—and I think it's great; I think our current situation is great—because out of this chaos, there's only one hope, and that's Jesus Christ. And I think every Christian is called to evangelize. . . . I'm preaching to you."

He did not have in mind evangelization through the construction of a biblical view of economics. He meant "tract-passing." He said that the Bible teaches that we cannot please our fellow man, that we can expect persecution (and he expects to be persecuted), and that hope is secured in this world through suffering. He said he is certain about the following facts. He is called, first, to exercise the Great Commission to witness to people about Christ. Second, he has a spiritual gift to be exercised in the body of Christ. Third, he is called to exercise spiritual leadership in his family. "Those three things I know for sure. What other things I have to do in this economy [dispensation?] I'm not sure of." In short, he must devote himself to *personal evangelism*, the *institutional church*, and his *family*. The rest of life he is not sure about.

This is the theology of pietism. It is the theology of external defeat. You do not win battles on battlefields where you are not quite sure you ought to be fighting. Yet he concluded his testimony with the statement: "I want to use my economic knowledge to glorify God."

What we can say is that his eschatology, his view of biblical law, and his willingness to de-emphasize his task as an economist, are all of one piece. His outlook is shared by the vast majority of those who call themselves Bible-believing Christians. His outlook is shared by the majority of those who teach in the Christian classrooms at the college level.

When one of the participants at this conference (who has an M.A. in economics) began teaching on a Baptist campus by announcing that he intended to teach an explicitly biblical economics, the students were astounded. Some even transferred to his class who had not originally intended to. They had never heard of such a thing. As far as most Christian campuses are concerned, the theology of retreat has accomplished the goals of the secularists: to snuff out the life-giving, society-reconstructing message of Christ to the whole of man's existence. (Not having a Ph.D., he was not given tenure in the department; in fact, his temporary position was soon to be filled by someone else.) When secular accrediting agencies can keep the comprehensive gospel out of Christian colleges, it's a testimony to the power of Satan, not of God. Satan wins the compromises. His most valuable accomplices are the Christian compromisers. You don't win confidence or battles when the first piece of equipment ordered by your troop commanders is a white flag.

10

SUBSIDIZING
GOD'S OPPONENTS

**"Below-cost tuitions are the *bribe offers* paid to
parents to send their kids to a politically alien
institution, and *unsuspecting church members
are supposed to finance the bribes.*"**

When a Christian begins to consult the Bible and
discovers the comprehensive claims that the Bible
places on Christ's followers, he steadily discovers
how many of Christ's opponents want him to finance
rival callings. The most glaring example today is the
government (public) school movement. Everyone is
compelled to support the spread of so-called neutral
education, meaning the religion of secular humanism. The funds are coerced from Christian parents.
Then, in many cases, parents are penalized for sending their children to a Christian school. The secular
humanists demand that the Christians use State-
approved textbooks, hire State-certified teachers,

and teach State-approved curricula. If the schools refuse, they lose their accreditation or their tax exemption. In some cases, pastors and school administrators, as well as parents, have been sent to jail for refusing to comply. If you think I am exaggerating, get some back issues of the *CLA Defender*, the publication of the Christian Law Association. Send a few dollars to CLA Defender, P.O. Box 30290, Cleveland, OH 44130.

The serious Christian eventually begins to figure out that he is being asked to finance his own destruction, not to mention the destruction of his children. Not only is he being asked to do this, he is being told to do it, on threat of imprisonment. And far too many Christians capitulate, though the ranks of those who won't are growing.

In other cases, the conflict is not so clear-cut. Within the institutional church, there are rival positions. These rival groups can sometimes gain control of the churches' various subcommittees or peripheral organizations. Christians can be found on both sides of a particular question. The problem arises when one group claims to have lawful access to the other side's tithes and offerings, to be used primarily for the benefit of the group's activities and goals. Immediately, there are conflicts. Who gets what? On what criteria? For how long? Will there be quotas set up? Will my group be allowed to get into the other group's share of the contributions? Do they contribute their fair share? What is a fair share? Have they been continuing over the years to give their fair share? Can we compel them to give their fair share in the future? What kind of institutional penalties can we impose if they refuse to contribute their fair share in the future?

These are not hypothetical. Questions like these are always sources of conflict in any organization, including institutional churches. It should be the goal of peace-keepers to set up institutional buffers and barriers to such conflicts. Smoothing over conflicts is one of the most important functions of a price system. To the extent that churches ignore the price mechanism, they will produce more conflicts than would otherwise have been necessary.

EDUCATION   One of the obvious sources of conflict in any church is the question of educating the children. First, should the institutional church be involved at all? People debate this fervently. Second, how should a school be financed? Third, who will screen the teachers? Fourth, which students will be allowed in? These are hard questions.

At the level of the elementary school, the issues are easier to resolve. The basic curriculum is fairly well agreed upon. The students should be taught the fundamental skills of literacy and computation. They may also be assigned Bible lessons. The debates between rival schools of theology are less intense, or appear to be, in the case of simple Bible stories. So the debate over screening of teachers is subdued, and it tends to focus on teaching competency, that is, on the teacher's ability to impart seemingly neutral, agreed-upon skills.

The higher we go up the grade ladder, the more

likely we will find conflict. People don't agree about government, history, economics, sex education, and so forth. Unless the school teaches only math, and perhaps some chemistry and physics, parents will disagree. If the church is involved in any way, other members may be brought into the debate, since their funds are involved. Finally, teachers may organize, or the administration may rebel. It can be very ugly.

The easiest, least wasteful way to solve this kind of conflict is to separate the school from the church, while simultaneously adopting the policy of charging full-cost tuitions. If the church or churches want to get involved with a particular school, it will be possible only indirectly, through financing scholarships for deserving children (families). The church can choose not to permit its scholarship funds to be spent in a particular local school if the conflict between church and school is great enough. But the price system tends to resolve the conflict most efficiently. Anyone who doesn't like the educational product needn't pay. He can shop around. Christ's institutional monopoly, the church, need not become tyrannical in areas like curriculum policy or teacher screening.

Unfortunately, church officers in the twentieth century have not been trained to think in such terms. The question of full-cost tuitions is not a chapter in a denomination's handbook for deacons, especially since the denominations do not have handbooks for deacons. So churches rush in where private entrepreneurs fear to tread, and the result is conflict.

HIGHER EDUCATION If the conflict over curricula
is heavy at the high school level, consider the problems of the college. (I do not mention universities,
since I am aware of no denomination-sponsored
Protestant or Reformed university.) The faculties
are hired for many reasons, but pleasing parents is
low on the list, if it is on the list at all. They are hired
because someone has earned a Ph.D. at some secular, atheist university, or because the Administration
wants people of a particular political philosophy—
generally, a philosophy not shared by the rank and
file of the denomination's laymen—or because a
department chairman wants a colleague who shares
his ideological outlook. But conforming faculty philosophies to the outlook of the bulk of the school's
financial supporters is not, by any stretch of the im-
agination, anything that a college Administration in-
tends to do.

In a market situation, the seller of a service must
conform himself to the demands of the buyers. If he
fails to do this, he goes bankrupt. But the academic
world has a shield against this pressure from the "un-
washed": tax-exempt status. If the college Administration can convince outside donors to cover the
deficit, then the college can teach what it wants, as
long as it can offer an academic degree which buyers
believe will entitle them (or their children) to lifetime
monopoly economic returns. Max Weber, the great
German social scientist, was correct when he observed over 60 years ago: "When we hear from all
sides the demand for an introduction of regular curricula and special examinations, the reason behind it

is, of course, not a suddenly awakened 'thirst for education' but the desire for restricting the supply for those positions and their monopolization by the owner of educational certificates." What parents really want for their children is money, other things being equal. They want a "white collar union card."

But who will pay the freight? *Rich alumni*, if the school is an older one, or a very prestigious Ivy League school. The *Federal government*, if the Administration is willing (as too many of them are) to compromise their morals and their theology, and beg for other people's confiscated tax money. Besides, all they have to give up is the right to mention God or the Bible in the buildings constructed with Federal dollars. A small price to pay, if you're an administrator. Better a new gym and no prayers, than no gym and the right to mention the name of God. First things first, you know.

The Christian colleges have another source of funds: *the denomination*. They can continue to keep tuition levels low if church officers will use part of the money collected in God's name and the moral requirement of the tithe to finance the politically liberal professors in their tenured safety. Then the steady indoctrination of the students can continue, all financed by parents and church members who do not share either the political outlook or the tenured safety of the college's faculty members.

The denomination ought to tell the college to charge full-cost tuitions. Why subsidize a long-term *investment* made by middle class and upper middle class parents for their children's financial futures?

But what about poor families with bright chilren? Well, what about them? Why not set up a denomination-operated college scholarship fund, with tax-deductible donations from those with money for the sake of the poor? Why must the college be subsidized directly?

I'll tell you why: because the college administrators know that many parents would refuse to send their children to the Keynesian or Freudian dominated college if they were required to pay full-cost tuitions. They would send their children to other less liberal or less expensive institutions. The college administrators know that *below-cost tuitions are the means of buying parental loyalty*, even though the parents know that the children will be compelled to run through the gauntlet of political liberalism in the social science and humanities departments. Below-cost tuitions are the *bribe offers* paid to parents to send their kids to a politically alien institution, and *unsuspecting church members are supposed to finance the bribes*. That way, the college's administrators can avoid having to staff the faculties in terms of what parents would really want *if* they had to pay the full cost of educating their children. All the college administrators have to do is to convince a handful of church officials to finance the deficit of the college, rather than set up a church scholarship program (where students could take their scholarships to competing colleges—perish the horrifying thought). So the silent laymen continue to finance the tenured political liberals in their positions of safety from parental demands.

CONCLUSION Is your church playing this game? If so, what do you think you can do to remedy the situation? When?

And if your denomination is financing another denomination's liberal-dominated faculty, then you had better make some changes soon. Just because a group of political liberals once earned Ph.D.'s doesn't mean that conservative laymen have a moral obligation to support them in their tenure-protected security.

11

THE STALEMATE MENTALITY

"Those who go into battle expecting defeat are soon defeated."

On December 7, 1941, the Japanese bombed Pearl Harbor. As one ship sat burning in the harbor, its anti-aircraft guns blazing at the incoming waves of planes, a chaplain reportedly began assisting the gunners, and was heard to shout, "Praise the Lord, and pass the ammunition!" This phrase was turned into a popular patriotic song of the Second World War. The chorus ended, "Praise the Lord, and pass the ammunition, and we'll all stay free." It was this vision of men's responsibilities that motivated British and American forces. Churchill's "Blood, Sweat, and Tears" speech — actually, he had said "blood, sweat, toil, and tears" — delivered a similar message: *the assurance of victory*, at first in a defensive battle, but ultimately offensively. The Allies were determined to carry the war to the enemy's front door, and then knock down the door. It would not be easy, but it would be done.

PUSAN OR INCHON?   In June of 1950, the North Korean army attacked South Korea. The poorly equipped South Korean army, outnumbered two-to-one, collapsed immediately. Half of its 65,000 men were killed, wounded, or taken prisoner. President Singman Rhee (age 75) and General Douglas MacArthur (age 74), who had flown in from Japan, watched the final rout from the front lines. Seoul, the South Korean capital, fell in four days.

America flew in the Army's 24th and 25th divisions from Japan. Inexperienced, poorly trained, and poorly equipped, they retreated for six weeks until they were trapped on the southern tip of Korea, the Pusan peninsula. Some American troops had surrendered at first, until they learned how few prisoners the North Koreans took. It looked as if MacArthur's troops would be pushed into the sea. Finally, the Americans and South Koreans dug in, and a stalemate ensued. A chunk of land south of a 120-mile strip across the southern tip of Korea was all that remained of free South Korea. Now what?

MacArthur had an idea. Why not lauch an invasion at the port of Inchon, 24 miles west of Seoul and 150 miles from the rear of the North Korean forces? It was considered impossible to complete an amphibious landing at Inchon. MacArthur knew what military experts believed, so he decided to attempt it. The element of surprise was crucial. The 1st Marine Division was secretly shipped in from San

Francisco, and on September 15, the invasion began.
It was over the day it started. The American forces
cut the North Koreans off from behind, and within
two weeks the North Koreans were defeated. Half
were in prisoner of war camps; the rest were cut off
in small units or trying to flee home.

The war did not end, of course. The Chinese
Communists invaded with a huge force of 300,000
men in late November. MacArthur had been caught
off guard, despite warning signs. The Chinese had
done to him what he had done to the North Koreans.
It was the worst military defeat of his career. He
learned first-hand what he had taught: there is no
respite during a war. *The war goes on until one side wins*.

The 1st Marine Division was cut off and surrounded.
They had attacked the Chinese from the rear, since
they had been 40 miles to the north when the
Chinese hit the Eighth Army. But the Chinese had
anticipated the Marines' attack, and had cut them
off. The Marines then broke out of the trap. Lt.
Gen. Walton Walker, the Marine commander, ut-
tered the classic line of the Korean war — which later
became the title of a movie about the war. When
asked by a reporter if he was retreating, he responded:
"*Retreat, hell! We're only attacking in a different direction.*"
Col. Lewis B. "Chesty" Puller almost matched
Walker's line: "The enemy is in front of us, behind
us, to the left of us, and to the right of us. They won't
escape this time." They hacked their way out for 14
days through blizzards and thousand-foot chasms.
(See William Manchester, *The Glory and the Dream*
[Boston: Little, Brown, 1972], pp. 530-47.)

"BUGOUT FEVER" Why all this military history in a book about religion? Because we are still in a war. From time to time, a truce breaks out. No one is fooled except the Christians. The old fundamentalism's equivalents of the State Department—seminaries, non-denominational magazines, old-line campus evangelism ministries, Gospel quartets, prophetic tape ministries, and paperback devotional books by housewives—keep informing us that the "real battle to come" is not for us, that the Tribulation is for the Jews, and victory is post-tribulation. Today's battle cry: "Pray for a stalemate." The largest Christian army on the field is an army of insurance salesmen selling eternal fire insurance policies to the terminal generation. The troops are all looking forward to R&R: not rest and recreation, but rapture and restoration. They suffer from the affliction first described at Pusan: *"bugout fever."* In 1950, American troops trapped at Pusan wanted to get back to Japan. Today, the Christian troops want to "bug out" to heaven before enemy forces launch the great Tribulation.

Those who promote "the last outpost" perspective are divided. Some believe that the last outpost will end with the return of Christ and His angels in final judgment. Conclusion: not a single non-ecclesiastical institution we build today will survive the final onslaught of the enemy, which precedes Christ's victorious return. The other major viewpoint teaches that Christ will return to set up an international chain of command with headquarters in Jerusalem. God's angels—a kind of heavenly "1st Airborne Division"—will relieve us of command, letting us "bug out" for our long-awaited R&R. When we return in our perfect physical bodies, it will be desk jobs, PX prices, and field-grade commissions for all of us, and hard times for spiritual gooks, wogs, and fuzzy-wuzzies everywhere, for a thousand years.

We all know one thing: *We're in Pusan*. We *are* trapped on the peninsula, and the enemy is at the bridges (or gates, as the case may be). Christians know that humanists control the Congress, the President, the big-three T.V. networks, the prestige universities, the public schools (except, you understand, local public schools attended by 90% of the children of the mainline denominations, where 30% of the faculty and the assistant football coach are Baptists, and it doesn't matter who writes the textbooks, so "go, team, go"), the news media (except, of course, the local newspaper, which is owned by a Presbyterian elder, and it doesn't matter who writes the AP and UPI stories), the social welfare committees of every denomination of more than 15,000 members, the oil companies, big business, big labor, and the big foundations. What do Christians control? The right-to-life movement, the temperance movement, half a dozen 4-year colleges, several satellite T.V. networks, and possibly as many as 14 small-town branches of the YMCA. This is Pusan. Will we break out or bug out?

Gen. MacArthur had the right idea: the Inchon landing. Gen. Walker also had the right idea: attacking in a different direction. Senior officers do not go into battle expecting to surrender, or to be trapped in some enclave. Those who do go into battle expecting defeat are soon defeated. They spend the war in a POW camp. Or the Gulag Archipelago.

WALKING THE POINT In mid-September of 1982, Rev. Jerry Falwell devoted one broadcast of his Old Time Gospel Hour to a report on the attacks he had sustained from the humanist media and humanist demonstrators. He showed film clips of placard-carrying protestors. He also showed filmed interviews with several of them. One group of protestors was parading in front of his church, and one of them carried a small cross with a dead frog nailed to it. The cross bore the inscription: "He died for your sins." To put it mildly, the protestors we saw were not people who inspire confidence.

The object of the presentation was to raise money. The various ministries of the Old Time Gospel Hour were under financial pressure, he reported. Giving was down, costs were up. With a 5,000-student college, the television programming costs, and all the other expenses, his ministry needs a continuing flood of money. The recession and the bad publicity had cut into people's giving, he reported.

The way he chose to raise funds is a good one: identify the common enemies. Provide visual proof of just how reprehensible the enemies are—the same thing humanists do when they run their full-page ads against the Moral Majority and related ministries. Books like *Holy Terror: The Fundamentalist War on America's Freedoms in Religion, Politics and Our Private Lives* (Doubleday, 1982), and *The New Subversives: Anti-Americanism of the Religious Right* (Continuum,

1982) pull no punches. But their humanist authors resent it when Falwell fights back for what *he* believes in.

A recurring theme in his presentation was this: "I am the point man in this battle." What is a point man? He is the soldier who walks ahead of the platoon, checking out the road, watching for the enemy, and drawing the first shots. He used another analogy: walking through the mine field. He might have used a third: a lightning rod. Someone has to walk the point, draw the initial fire, catch the flak. Jerry Falwell is the New Christian Right's point man.

Obviously, most soldiers prefer not to walk the point. It is a dangerous position. There is nowhere to hide when you walk the point. This is the job which he has chosen, he said, and he is willing to continue. But, he said, he wants to know that others are behind him, that they will take a stand with him. *No one wants to walk the point if the troops behind him have retreated.*

This leads me to the following observation: if he is going to survive the ordeal, the point man needs a team backing him up. But if the team is to be motivated to do this, rather than bug out, the members need to have confidence. They need to trust their commanding officer, their noncommissioned officer, and their point man. They also need to trust their battle plan. A platoon that expects to be wiped out probably will be. No point man wants to walk the point in front of a discouraged platoon that is ready to cut and run at the first sound of gunfire.

What impressed me about Rev. Falwell's appeal was this: he kept telling his viewers that victory is assured, that the forces of moral righteousness will not be defeated, that the United States is about to be turned around. *Like a good company commander, he was talking victory.* He was rallying the troops for a fight. He was not calling them to a losing battle.

The "electronic churchmen" who are trying to rally Christians to take a stand have abandoned the language of premillennialism. Those who still cling tightly to the older faith are not calling their viewers to do anything risky, or to take an unpleasant stand. The difference between the preaching of Howard C. Estep ("The King is Coming") and Jerry Falwell is striking. The latter has not officially abandoned the eschatology of the former, but unofficially he preaches a new gospel, a gospel of victory.

What the New Christian Right has discovered is that if this society isn't redeemed, then we face a cultural crisis of major proportions. They have built up large followings, have amassed huge debts, and they now face political and ultimately religious pressures from the humanists who dominate the media and national politics. They see the need of fighting back, but they have learned an important truth: *it is difficult to raise troops and money for a losing cause.* It is easier for followers to stay home and play safe, when it is a question of getting behind a point man in a self-professed losing cause. And the point men like Falwell who refuse to quit now need to rally the troops.

They are no longer calling for an enclave, for a

perpetual stalemate. They are no longer content to remain bottled up on the Pusan peninsula. No one needs a point man in a defensive operation anyway; point men are offensive. They are used in breakouts. They are used to "carry the war to the enemy." They are not used in defensive operations. *By identifying himself as a point man, Jerry Falwell has been forced, institutionally and financially, to abandon the language of premillennial dispensationalism, whether he still believes it or not.* He has adopted the language of victory.

Christians are rallying to support Falwell and others like him who stand up and fight. In doing so, they are steadily abandoning premillennialism, psychologically if not officially.

Older groups still cling to eschatologies of defeat. These groups are large, but they are dying. Their influence is shrivelling up. People who have rallied for a battle do not want to hear tales of inevitable defeat from their commanders.

The kind of theology represented by Hal Lindsey's books is fading. Those who believe Lindsey hope for "peace in Pusan." *They pray for a continuing stalemate*, for they see persecution and external defeat as the only alternative to stalemate. But those people are not in the front lines of today's religious battles. *"Bugout theology" does not produce armies, only refugees.* These people cannot serve as point men. Their theology will not produce a sustained battle — the kind of battle Christians are lining up for today.

A stalemate is not good enough. MacArthur said it best: *"There is no substitute for victory."*

12

WHAT KIND OF ARMY?

"An army which is told that it must suffer defeat, that any sign of victory is an illusion or else a lure into a subsequent defeat, that victory must be the Devil's, will be a *defeated army*."

"Onward, Christian Soldiers" is a favorite hymn of most people. It is far better known than "Wayfaring Stranger," which begins: "I am a poor wayfaring stranger, just travelling through this world of woe." Yet the sentiments of the vast majority of professing Christians are with the second song, despite the fact that they are not very poor, and they are travelling in very fine style. The pilgrim motif is a lot more popular than the soldier motif.

There are reasons for this. "Christian," in John Bunyan's classic seventeenth-century allegory, *Pilgrim's Progress*, was basically an unemployed drifter before he was converted, and an unemployed traveller after. What did the man do for a living? Like the radio and television character of the 1940's and early 1950's, Ozzie Nelson, he had no visible means of support, no calling. Ozzie, however, must have done something for a living, but "Christian" just plodded on and on through life. Bunyan, a wandering tinker for much of his life, and imprisoned for most of the remainder, to some degree resembled "Christian." But a tinker at least faced a market and delivered valuable services; "Christian" was, as far as we can see, a vagrant.

This pilgrim motif stresses internal struggles over sin, rather than struggles with external enemies. The soldier motif is the opposite. The soldier gains his self-confidence and skills in boot camp; after this initial training, he is assumed to be ready for battle. He concerns himself with the enemy, who is a true threat to his life. The pilgrim is more like a newly reformed alcoholic, or a drug addict going "cold turkey." He wails, groans, writhes, struggles with inner horrors, and concentrates on what is going on inside him. He is at war with himself and his flesh, but not primarily at war with the external environment. The various allegorical characters in *Pilgrim's Progress* are external representations of internal enemies: vanity, doubt, despair, and so forth. The pilgrim does not bother much with his external environment, since he is only passing through. The soldier, on the other hand, is a conqueror, and he has to be concerned with what is going on around him.

Perhaps the most detailed pilgrim manual is William Gurnall's *The Christian in Complete Armor*, the seventeenth-century book which devotes its 2,000 pages to a consideration of every conceivable personal temptation faced by the soul—except, unfortunately, the temptations of the battlefield. Gurnall did not involve himself in the theological battles of the day, which were literally life-and-death battles, and he signed the Act of Uniformity in 1662, thereby insuring his continued income as a State-certified pastor, while 2,000 Puritan ministers refused to sign and were thrown out of their pulpits and, in many cases, into jail. Gurnall preferred a life of irrelevance, warring with his own internal lusts, ignoring the external civil issues of his day. However harrowing his internal battles may have been, this pilgrim made his journey through his enrivonment in comfort and relative safety.

THE BATTLEFIELD People get shot on battlefields. They get hurt. They aren't paid much, and what little they have is at perpetual risk. They can count on little from their external environment. They rely on their own wits, their past training, their experience under fire, their army supply system, and, most of all, the success of their commanding officer. The best-executed battle plan can lead to disaster if it is not the appropriate battle plan. The stakes are high, yet the foot soldier must act in faith, obedient to his commanders, whether or not the plan is well-designed. The chain of command must function all the time, if it is to function at all.

Cromwell's forces knew this, and they were nearly invincible on the battlefield. Cromwell was a military genius, an innovative cavalry officer, and a forceful leader of men. They trusted his military skills, they executed his plans, and they toppled the British monarchy in the mid-seventeenth-century. When the New Model Army went into action, it was a true army.

Yet once the war was over, the splintering began. There was no real unanimity of goals and methods during Cromwell's Protectorate. Men knew what they had to do to survive on the battlefield, but in peacetime, the unifying enthusiasms, as well as the unifying fear of military defeat, disappeared.

It is much the same today, except today's Christians have allegorized the language of battle. They have bled and died in the wars of humanistic imperialism, but they no longer understand, or even recognize the validity of, the legitimately Christian battle. They have spiritualized and internalized the Bible's language of warfare. They are not willing to step out into a real battlefield, since they have never experienced boot camp. They are not fit for a war.

Aleksandr Solzhenitsyn's *Gulag Archipelago* makes it clear that a war is on, and that Christians are deeply involved. The same point is made by Kourdakov's *The Persecutor* and Richard Wurmbrand's *Tortured for Christ*. In Communist China, the persecution after 1949 may have been even worse, as Raymond de Jaeger's *The Enemy Within* indicates. Real battles, real life-and-death decisions, are being made in real battlefields, daily, all over the world. Nevertheless, American Christians cannot recognize the signs of battle. They cannot even recognize the threat posed to them by the public school system. They co-operate. They go along. They worry about the allegorical battles, not the real ones. Whether or not a county allows the sale of alcoholic beverages is a major issue in the South's more rural counties; whether or not to start a Christian school isn't, for the vast majority of Baptists and Methodists. They battle pink elephants, while sacrificing their children, tuition free, to the Moloch State.

"Shoot a Commie for Christ" is a slogan of ridicule used by secularists to impugn the motives of Christians. Yet the escalation of war tensions may make it necessary for Americans to be asked by their government to "Shoot a Commie for America." They did in the Grenada invasion in 1983. We have been asked to "shoot a kraut for Britain" twice in this century. What we take as a national duty — service to the humanist State — we regard as ridiculous in the field of religion. The holy wars of this century have been the most devastating, most ferocious wars in man's history, but the holy gods have been the humanist gods of the State and Party. Armies were once asked to go into battle in the name of a transcendental God, but whole populations today are called to self-sacrifice and self-immolation in the name of the *Volk*, the Proletariat, and the Fatherland.

THE CHAIN OF COMMAND What modern Christians object to is the idea of an earthly chain of command. To some extent, the Mormons still believe in the idea, although I doubt that every Mormon has bought a year's supply of food for each member of the family, which is what they have been instructed to do. Roman Catholics acknowledge the legitimacy of a chain of command, but most of them practice contraception, in direct violation of the Pope's orders. In other words, even those who say they believe in a chain of command are willing to acknowledge its legitimacy only when the chain of command refuses to enforce fundamental law. This is a century of *conformity to the State*, not conformity to the church.

Men will conform. It is a question of which agency or agencies will gain the subordination of the population. In Protestant circles, the chain of command has generally become mush, because it is cut off at the top (as in Baptist and Congregationist circles), or because it has become bureaucratized (the denominations). The people have no real confidence in their elected elders, their seminary-trained pastors, and their collection plate-passing deacons. While some local churches may operate in rather strict conformity to the wishes of a dynamic pastor, this dedication is generally not transferable to his successor, indicating that there was no real chain of command. There was only the strong personality of one leader—a leader who may have refused to delegate basic decisions to subordinates in the first place.

Protestants are not used to exercising authority, probably because they are unwilling to accept the legitimacy of ecclesiastical authority. Any church hierarchy which attempts to exact conformity from recalcitrant members will face the inevitable competition of another church, right down the street, which opens its arms to any disaffected member who will transfer his membership and his tithe (or what pitiful giving Protestants have substituted for a tithe). The competition is too stiff, and the competition has led to a least-common-denominator chain of command.

What kind of army functions without a chain of command? None. Then what kind of army is the church? A defeated army. An army which is told that it must suffer defeat, that any sign of victory is an illusion or else a lure into a subsequent defeat, that victory must be the Devil's, will be a *defeated army*. Yet this is precisely what modern Christians have been told, and since they don't like the rigors of battle, and since they don't like the discipline of a chain of command, and since they really don't trust the judgment of their officers, they prefer to listen to stories of defeat. Defeatism justifies their own softness. And since they are guaranteed victory in the internal battles (they think), and since the external warfare is simply allegorical (they think), they can dismiss as ridiculous the idea that we really should be training as cultural soldiers — soldiers ready to do battle on a multitude of battlefields.

THE SUPREME COMMANDER Jesus Christ is our supreme commander, but He operates only through His word, which is unquestionably a training manual. However, He has many interpreters, and few people see the Bible as a true training manual. There are too many one-star generals in a peacetime army, all building up their local empires, all jealously competing against their peers, and most of them completely unprepared for a war. When the war comes, both superiors and inferiors recognize which generals are fit to lead, and the peacetime bureaucrats are rapidly removed from public scrutiny. Peacetime armies cannot tolerate men like Patton, or even MacArthur;

in a shooting war, you cannot win without them.

Field-grade officers—majors and colonels—are numerous. (A seminary professor is a light colonel.) That's what Protestants have in large numbers. However, they all have the idea that they are generals, or if not actually generals, then at least they are as good as today's generals. They know for sure that nobody is about to follow them into battle, so it really doesn't make much difference how good or incompetent they are. Nobody recognizes that the war is on, because it's not a shooting war yet.

Second lieutenants are, as always, as expendable as tent pegs, and not much more useful. They are the deacons, seminarians, and elders in churches that are one-man bands. They know they are unprepared, and so does everyone else. Noncommissioned officers, such as Sunday School teachers, are ignored by everyone. They are assumed to be incompetent, but you need them in any bureaucratic system. We supply them with weak or corrupted materials, give them no training, and send them out to teach. Teach what? Well, whatever drivel pietistic evangelicals have published, or whatever socialistic, guilt-producing handbooks that have been issued by the denomination's liberals.

The troops sit passively, confused, unaware that a war is in progress. They think their commanders are on top of everything. They don't even feel called upon to exercise minimal leadership, which is just what their superiors prefer.

We have no strategists, so far as I can determine. How could we? We haven't won a major battle in this century. (When was the last time a theological liberal was removed for heresy by any American church, other than by the Missouri Synod Lutherans, in this century?)

We have a few tacticians who have specialized in areas like starting Christian schools, or battling against abortion, or setting up small activist or publishing organizations, but their efforts are not coordinated, and they seldom respect any single leader. Even communications are lacking; the groups seldom talk to each other.

If we have any generals, nobody salutes them, especially bird colonels, who generally think that *they* are the true generals.

THE WAR When war comes—persecution, a Soviet victory, rioting in the streets, more visible attacks on Christian schools, a gun confiscation law, an economic collapse—then the generals will appear. There will be leaders only when the followers see the strategic necessity of following. When external conditions make mandatory a chain of command, we will see its creation.

We already have a reliable Supreme Commander. He knows what has to be done to win. His enemies cannot defeat Him or His troops. When commanders who are capable of leading join forces with followers who trust their judgment and who are willing to sacrifice for the sake of the war, we will see the light. And books on the inevitability of external defeat will no longer be best sellers. Psychological losers who don't understand the stakes of this war are the buyers of such books. They will not survive the first volley.

13

PROGRESSIVE RESPONSIBILITY

". . . we are the recipients of a law structure which is the proper foundation for all our personal decisions."

The apostle Paul recognized the necessity of Christians exercising leadership, first within the Christian community, and later in the very processes of the cosmos. When the sin-plagued Corinthian church faced a major disciplinary problem, Paul wrote to them that they should handle it themselves. They should not appeal to a secular law court, he said, implying that since the court would not be governed by the standards of biblical law, it would be a poor testimony to seek judgment there. It was wrong in principle because it would appear to sanction the validity of Satan's rule over the church. "Do ye not know that the saints shall judge the world? and if the world shall be judged by you, are ye unworthy to judge the smallest matters" (I Cor. 6:2)? Not only will the saints judge the world, they will also judge the angels, Paul said. If we shall judge the angels, "how much more things that pertain to this life" (I Cor. 6:3b)?

To humble them, and to demonstrate how important it was for them to stay out of the civil courts, Paul advised them: "If then ye have judgments of things pertaining to this life, set them to judge who are least esteemed in the church" (I Cor. 6:4). In other words, the least esteemed member of the local church was far better fit to make a valid judgment of the dispute than the high officials in the civil courts. As Paul said in the next sentence, "I speak to your shame. Is it so, that there is not a wise man among you? No, not one that shall be able to judge between his brethren" (I Cor. 6:5)? Paul really preferred that they find a competent, experienced man of judgment within the congregation. He did not really want the least esteemed man to judge. But he had made his point: better the least esteemed man in the church— someone who would not normally be regarded as a reliable ruler—than a civil magistrate in Corinth.

GOOD LAW, INEXPERIENCED JUDGES What we should understand from the beginning is that we are the recipients of a law structure which is the proper foundation for all our personal decisions. This law structure has been designed to fit the external realm of human action. It has been designed by God to provide a productive order. When men are exposed to the preaching of the whole counsel of God, they are able to begin to make valid distinctions between right and wrong. They can begin to deal with the sins in their own lives, and from there they can begin to handle the sin-created disputes in the local church. So reliable is the law of God, that Paul could tell the Corinthians that the least esteemed man in the church, with only a vague conception of the proper application of biblical law, was a more preferable judge than the master of humanistic law in the local Corinthian court. Better to subject oneself to an inexperienced judge who has a vague understanding of God's revelation than to be judged by a skilled lawyer who is not guided by the precepts of biblical law. That is how much more reliable the law of God is than the humanistic laws of the pagan civil governments.

Paul was not writing to citizens of a Christian political order. He was not saying that there should be no civil government, either. He himself appealed to Caesar when he believed his case was being handled improperly (Acts 25:11). However, his dispute was not with members of the church in this case. When he wrote to church members who were living in a pagan political order, which meant a pagan religious order, he advised them to create an alternative order, a Christian order in which their disputes with each other would not be revealed to the pagans around them, and in which these disputes might be resolved peacefully in terms of a revealed law-order. He warned them not to submit their institutional disputes for judgment to a representative of a rival institutional order. They were not to allow themselves to be dominated by their religious opponents, whose commitment was to other gods and other law-orders.

Would this not create problems within the church? Obviously, the problems were there already. It was a question of how to solve these problems with the least display of subservience to the pagan world. It was the responsibility of the members to become skilled in settling disputes in the local church. Until this was done, there was no way that they could come before the pagans of their day to announce a new king, with a new law-order. They could not begin to exercise dominion over the face of the earth if their own internal conflicts were being settled by representatives of an enemy law-order. They were not supposed to subordinate themselves before a rival law court, except in a case in which the members of the pagan civil order had unrighteously brought charges against them, or were trying to defraud them. In such a case, they might legitimately go to court, since there was no way to compel the members of pagan society to submit to the judgment of the church court.

THEOCRACY VS. ECCLESIOCRACY Was Paul arguing for some sort of ecclesiocracy? Was he trying to get the whole world under the authority of church courts? Did he envision a day in the future when everyone will be a church member, and the church courts will take the place of the despised civil courts? Paul never said so. What Paul was arguing for was *theocracy*—the rule of God's law. He was *not* arguing for ecclesiocracy, meaning civil rule by priests or ministers. He did see that it was better to settle disputes among church members without appealing to a rival religious order to restore peace. Yet in Romans 13:1-7, he acknowledged the legitimacy of civil rulers. He even called them ministers. Paul's theology held that there are two basic ministerial offices, civil rulers and elders in the church. Neither is to replace the other. Neither can perform all the functions of the other. Neither is to be vested with comprehensive, monopolistic sovereignty. And both are to be governed by God's law.

His unwillingness to allow the Corinthian church to appeal to the civil magistrate was based on his understanding of the inherent rivalry between two competing law-orders. It was not a question of the separation of Church and State which undergirded his argument. In that era, the Corinthian church was not able to appeal to civil magistrates who were governed by the terms of biblical law. It was not that the church courts should always rule in disputes between Christians; it was that God's law should always rule in disputes between Christians; it was that God's law should have a monopoly of lawful authority in disputes between Christians. It was not that the civil law should be transformed into ecclesiastical law; it was that both ecclesiastical law and civil law should be conformed to God's law, with neither the church nor the State possessing an absolute monopoly of lawful authority.

Paul was not arguing for the rule of church courts over every area of life, but he was arguing against the concept of neutral law. If the saints will judge the world, then neutral law is a myth. A man must judge in terms of standards. An act is right or wrong, acceptable or prohibited. If Christians are to judge the angels, then they must do so within a framework of morality designed by God and revealed to man. The Corinthian Christians were to stay out of pagan law courts precisely because there is no neutral civil law. Civil law, like church law, is governed by religious presuppositions concerning morality. Religious civil law may be defended in terms of a philosophy of universal neutralism, but such an argument is itself intensely religious and unneutral, for there are irreconcilable conflicts between biblical law's grounding in God's revelation and any other law-order which is not grounded in His revelation. The judgment of this world by the saints testifies to the absence of neutral law and neutral lawyers or judges. It is the saints who are the judges, not the self-professed neutralists. There will be no neutrality on the day of judgment. It will be the universal rule of God's law which prevails.

GOOD LAW, EXPERIENCED JUDGES The Corinthians were to seek out the most competent judges within the membership of the church. They were to elevate these men to the seat of authority. These men, not pagan judges, were to be preferred by the members in the settlement of disputes.

Was Paul forever closing the door to an expansion of godly rule? He was not a defender of ecclesiocracy. He acknowledged the civil ruler's role as a minister of God. So what did he have in mind? How could the influence of the gospel be legitimately restricted to the institutional church? How could pagan magistrates continue to exercise dominion if and when the gospel spread across the land? With the triumph of the Christians in the affairs of Rome, both East (Byzantium) and West (Europe), the pagan civil magistrates were replaced by Christians, from the fourth century onward. Were the newly ordained Christian civil magistrates to govern in terms of the older pagan law-order—the very law-order that Paul had advised the Corinthians to avoid in every instance of intra-church conflict? Or were they instead to reconstruct the civil law-order to conform to biblical standards set forth for civil rule?

Paul was not trying to keep the Corinthian church in bondage to less experienced judges. He did tell them to find the best men to handle cases. But was he telling them to avoid dominion tasks like taking over positions in the civil government? He never said so. In fact, his strong emphasis on the reliability of godly rule by Christian leaders within the church —experienced, competent leaders if they could be located—testifies to his preference for competence. But his letter advised the Corinthians to seek first the rule of God's law, not human competence as such; only after the rule of God's law was agreed upon were they to seek out the most competent men to rule over them. It is God's law which has preeminence in judgement, not certified competence. Nevertheless, within the agreed-upon framework of Christian institutional rule, the best men are to be elevated to positions of authority. God's law, *then* competent judges: here is Paul's message to the church. Men's competence is to be attained by means of God's law. Technical competence in law is not to be preferred to biblical law, for there is no such thing as technical competence as such, or neutral law as such. *The standard is biblical law*, administered with or without great technical competence. Where are men to gain the preferred competence? Obviously, by becoming familiar with the terms of biblical law. First, they learn as *children* (Deut. 6:6-7). Second, they learn as *church members* in churches governed by elders who respect biblical law (I Cor. 6). Third, they learn as *deacons*, who assist the elders in the less crucial responsibilities, like the administration of charity (Acts 6:1-4). This office is a sort of apprenticeship position. Fourth, men may be appointed to the office of church *elder* (I Tim. 3). But this presumes that they have already approved themselves in the fifth office, that of *household head* (I Tim. 3:4-5), which is also a requirement for deacons (I Tim. 3:12).

This, however, is only the beginning. Men are also to serve in positions of authority in business, the military, medicine and other professions, the civil government, and wherever God's law applies. (It applies wherever men make decisions for which they are responsible before God; only in those zones of life for which men will never have to give an account of their actions—in the "neutral zones of life"—does biblical law not apply. Anyone who denies the rule of God's law must explain, using the Bible as his source, just where such zones are.) Men are to become competent rulers—judges, if you prefer—in their labor. *Their callings before God are training grounds for the exercise of godly judgment.*

CONCLUSION The doctrine that the church and its members will experience an endless series of failures until the day of judgment, whereupon the saints shall judge the world with Christ, has this curious implication: experience in exercising godly judgment is best attained through constant failure and the inability of saints to gain positions of authority, in time and on earth. In other words, Christians will *never* rule on earth, and *therefore* they *will* rule after the final judgment. Those Christians who argue that individual saints will be far removed forever from the seats of power or even the corridors of power, until the day of judgment itself, are building a theoretical case for the success of *off*-the-job training. They are arguing for perpetual childhood and subservience: domination by rebellious rulers—ever-more consistent, ruthless, and lawless rulers—is the way to become competent rulers. But the Bible tells us that a sign of God's judgment is to be ruled by children (Isaiah 3:4). We need an eschatology which offers us a doctrine of *progressive responsibility*, a doctrine of *maturing judgment*. We need a concept of *on-the-job training* and *promotion through competence*.

14

THE "LITTLE THINGS" OF LIFE

"It is the law-order imparted by parents to children which will determine the success or failure of a society."

Western civilization is the historical product of Christianity. Without Christianity, the development of the West would have been radically different. Of course, secular humanism and various intermediary philosophies have contributed greatly to the growth and shape of Western institutions since about 1660, but without the impact of Christian thought and culture, the foundations of Western secular humanism would not have been laid. It is impossible to think of Western culture without considering the historical impact of Christianity.

Most Protestants understand this fact. Yet at the same time, they have a tendency to denigrate the cultural accomplishments of the Roman Catholic

Church in the medieval era. It is as if Protestants think that Western culture sprang up overnight in response to Luther's nailing of the 95 theses on the door. But when we consider the savagery that faced the Irish missionaries in the sixth and seventh centuries, we all should become aware of the vast impact pre-Reformation Christianity had on Europe. In fact, without that impact, there would never have been a Europe. There would have been nothing more than pagan, fragmented tribes of primitive savages, with only an occasional raid from the Norsemen to bring "advanced" pagan culture into their lives.

There is little reason to believe that the level of formal Christian education was very great in pre-Reformation times. Without literacy and the printing press, written European culture was the possession of a tiny elite. What literacy that did exist prior to the eleventh century did so primarily in the monasteries, especially in Ireland. The knowledge of Christ and His work was overwhelmingly verbal, ritualistic, and visual, in the form of statues and architecture, with some painting. The fables, legends, hymns, Bible stories, and reworked pagan myths were mixed together in a complex form, with great regional and linguistic variations, to produce what we classify vaguely as medieval civilization. But it *was* civilization. It was not primitive. The cultural shambles left by Rome, after Rome had disintegrated, was reworked by Christians to become a full-fledged culture. (See, for example, William Carroll Bark's *Origins of the Medieval World* and Friedrich

Heer's *The Medieval World*, both available in inexpensive paperbacks.)

The question then arises: How was it that pre-Reformation religion could build up a new, thriving civilization, if the level of theological awareness was so minimal? How could it be that the confused mixtures of paganism, Bible stories, myths, relics, and all the other fragments of medieval Christianity could create the foundation, region by region, of a totally new civilization?

BIBLICAL LAW   It was primarily the rule of biblical law, not the influence of architecture, paintings, or even hymns, that reshaped European life prior to the Reformation _ was the restraining influence of law —family law, church law, business law, and civil law —that provided the West with a new vision. Rushdoony writes of the progress of law after the sixth century:

> Roman law now continued in its development, but it became progressively an expression of Biblical law. Justinian's *Institutes* (with the Digest, Code, and Novels, a part of the *Corpus Juris Civilis*) clearly reflects what is now called "natural law," but that concept was now becoming something other than Roman law had known. . . . Natural law, whether in the hands of jurists, scholastics, or Deists, was in essence an anti-trinitarian doctrine, but it was still more Christian than Roman. Natural law became a form of Christian heresy and ascribed

to nature the legislative powers and absolute laws which were clearly borrowed from the God of Scripture. Thus, both Roman law and natural law became so thoroughly Christianized with the centuries that no Roman would have recognized them. Even where the wording of ancient Roman laws was retained, a new content and interpretation rendered the ancient meaning remote and barren. ("Notes on the Law in Western Society," *The Institutes of Biblical Law* [Nutley, New Jersey: Craig Press, 1973], pp. 786-87.)

The spread of biblical law across the face of Europe served as an integrating factor. Sharing basic presuppositions, and sharing also a single written language (Latin), scholars throughout Europe had the tools for restructuring the face of society. Localism was basic to the political and even ecclesiastical institutions of medieval society, but there was also unity with respect to first principles. Applications were local, but the shared frame of reference allowed the intellectual and moral leaders of society to grapple with the affairs of life along similar lines. The division of intellectual labor could therefore be integrated. Each man's moral and intellectual efforts had more opportunity to be translated into action across the whole continent than would have been the case had there been no shared presuppositions. Men's intellectual efforts could therefore become cumulative. Biblical law redirected the paths of human endeavor, generation after generation, into channels that proved to be incredibly productive. Change was slow, but life was not stagnant.

THE FAMILY However important intellectual life is for a culture, the most important applications of morals, religion, and philosophy are found inside the family unit. This is the universal human institution. The family is the original agency of government, especially self-government. What families believe concerning their responsibilities before God is more important for the construction of a civilization than the attitudes of the members of any other institution. *It is the family unit which is central for the construction, or reconstruction, of civilization.*

When we think of the law of Moses, we should never forget the requirement of universal family instruction in biblical law: "And these words, which I command thee this day, shall be in thine heart: And thou shalt teach them diligently unto thy children, and shalt talk of them when thou sittest in thine house, and when thou walkest by the way, and when thou liest down, and when thou risest up" (Deut. 6:6-7). The enormous capital resources in time, effort, and personal concern that parents are to expend on their children's legal instruction cannot be overestimated as a factor in cultural and economic growth. Not the State, church, or school, but the family is to be central in legal education. The day-to-day instruction in righteousness which all child-rearing involves is the very heart of a civilization. *It is the law-order imparted by parents to children which will determine the success or failure of a society.*

This instruction may not be self-conscious on the part of parents. This instruction may be simply a series of commands, or punishments, that really is not an integrated program. If so, the children suffer, and the future is compromised. But all parents must instruct children in the law-order of the family, or else chaos results. Parents have a direct incentive to direct their children's footsteps. There can be no family unit without an integrating, disciplining law-order.

When we attempt to reconstruct mentally what local family life may have been like in the medieval world—which means a period of over a thousand years, and tens of thousands of little communities—we can barely imagine what went on. We have only the faintest shadows of the past. Medieval families did not leave written documents. But we know the results. Agriculture improved. New technologies were invented, capitalized, and exported. The population grew slowly, erratically, but universally, leading to the progressive cultivation of the soil. (See Lynn White, Jr., *Medieval Technology and Social Change* [Oxford University Press, 1966 edition].)

When we look at the results of a thousand years of Christian instruction, from 500 A.D. to 1500 A.D., we begin to perceive the effect of these millions and millions of seemingly infinitesimal additions of moral capital. From the disintegration of Rome until the Reformation, Christian parents built a civilization. However ignorant of theology they may have been, however erroneous in their perception of things spiritual, not to mention things scientific, they nevertheless succeeded in reshaping the history of mankind. Their ignorance did not keep them from outdistancing India, China, and the other ancient civilizations by the end of the medieval period. There was a *cumulative effect* of the vast number of successive additions of family capital: agricultural, technological, educational, and moral. Line upon line, precept upon precept, a body of moral capital was built up, and it produced a new civilization.

CONCLUSION However important theology may be, it is the *application* of that theology to specific instances of daily living that makes the difference culturally. Theology is not simply an affair of the educational specialists. Flourishing theology is always practical theology. Theology has implications for every sphere of human existence. It is basic to the successful outworking of God's dominion covenant (Gen. 1:28) that people begin to apply the truths they have learned, especially in family affairs. If theology is untranslated into the little things of life, then it is truncated theology—cut off at the root. If the construction of ever-more finely honed theological formulations does not lead to altered family, church, business, or school operations, then it is dead theology. It was not the incredibly erudite debates of late medieval scholasticism that built medieval culture. Indeed, these debates among the schoolmen were the sign of the strangulation of medieval culture, the end of the line for the medieval world.

Theological scholarship, apart from concrete applications, is dead scholarship that leads nowhere. If we are to interpret properly the enormous erudition and mathematical sophistication of today's academic scholarship, we must understand that the Alexandrian scholarship of the dying Classical world and the arcane debates of the late medieval world were testimonies to the death of culture, not a new beginning. The dead within the academic world are buried by others using highly polished spades, tools sharpened with such precision that they are suitable only for splitting academic hairs. It is the "little things" of life, restructured in terms of valid applied theology, not the "big things" of the hair-splitters, that determine the future of a civilization.

15

SHEPHERDS AND SHEEP

"The battle for Christian reconstruction is many-faceted, but there is a single "litmus test" to separate the shepherds from the soon-to-be-sheared sheep in this battle: their support, financial, familistic, and verbal, of the Christian day school movement."

Any successful strategy of conquest must employ a two-pronged attack: the grand design and specific tactics. We need to participate in a co-ordinated program of conquest. This is what Christians have never succeeded in achieving. The various Christian churches, not to mention independent groups not directly connected to denominations, have always arrogated to themselves almost total authority. They have not been able to co-operate in the realm of first principles, nor in the area of strategy. They have thought they could "go it alone."

The result has been fragmentation. This, however, is only part of the story. It is not just that denominations have not co-operated well. It is also that the individual churches have fragmented internally. The centralists have tended to become full-time bureaucrats seeking power, and the decentralized pastors, teachers, and other Christian workers have tended to go their own way, leaving the tedious affairs of central administration to those with a taste for it. Those with a taste for bureaucratic administration seldom have a taste for creeds, theology, and (nonhumanistic) innovation, all of which are controversial, and all of which tend to reduce the powers of bureaucracies. *Hierarchies have strangled culture-altering Christian innovation.*

What is needed is a working *federalism*, among Christian groups and within each group. What is needed is *decentralization*, yet with sufficient willingness on the part of the "eyes" to recognize the importance of the "feet," and with all acknowledging the authority of the "head," Jesus Christ (I Corinthians 12). We need *multiple responsibilities* governed by biblical revelation and the leading of the Holy Spirit. What is needed is a *vision of conquest so great that we must co-operate.*

The cost of gaining co-operation institutionally has proven prohibitively high for centuries. Churches haven't co-operated very often. They haven't agreed on policy, organization, and the assignment of tasks. Unquestionably, this has been an institutional failure on the part of institutional Christianity. The hands and feet have looked to an earthly head, and the Bible teaches that there is no head, except Christ. Roman Catholics cannot convince Protestants that the Pope is that head, and premillennialists cannot convince the others that Christ will return to earth for a thousand years prior to final judgment to serve as the earthly head. Almost everyone else has given up the vision of conquest because there is no earthly head. The fact must be faced: in time and on earth, as of the mid-1980's, there is no acceptable source of institutional strategy, no organizing general who is followed by all Christians. But never forget: the Satanists and humanists have no visible, earthly general, either.

THE COMMON ENEMY Christians are supposed to love each other. Communists are supposed to share bonds with all proletarians and other communists. Every ideological group proclaims universality, and all of them bicker internally, never displaying unity except in the face of a common enemy.

Humanism today is the common enemy of Christians. The Pentecostals are seeing this more and more clearly. The Roman Catholics who take the faith seriously cannot afford to waste time and energy worrying about merely heretical Protestants: they have too many apostate clerics and theologians to contend with. The Baptists, the Lutherans, and the handful of believing Episcopalians who are still inside their churches are besieged on every side by the enemy. The fact is simple: the enemy of all orthodoxy has surrounded the churches, and in most cases is already inside the gates. In too many instances, humanists are in the temple itself, setting policy in the seminaries, colleges, and Sunday school editorial committees. On all sides, Christians are surrounded by Unitarians (who may call themselves something else for the sake of their strategy).

What we find, therefore, is that those who are the great proponents of institutional centralization are almost always those who hold to a theology of political salvation. They want to centralize institutional power because they believe that mankind will be regenerated, and society purified, by means of the exercise of external force. In the division of labor, these people tend to get on top, for they do best what they are committed to, namely, exercising power.

What we are seeing today is a steady increase in awareness among thoughtful Christians that the common enemy, secular humanism, is a greater threat than the shades of theological emphasis separating them from other besieged Christians. They are beginning to understand that there have to be alternatives to the centralizing rot of political theology, humanism. They feel the impending doom of humanism's eroding civilization, and they are convinced that they must not go down with humanism's ship. A few — a very few, sadly — are trying to construct alternative vessels.

What are these alternative vessels? Prayer groups, missionary boards, Christian professional associations, tape libraries, publishing houses, and special interest associations, most notably the right-to-life societies. But one vessel stands out as the pre-eminent one: the independent Christian day school.

ALTERNATIVE EDUCATION The serious Christians who are convinced that the battle against humanism is the crucial battle of our age are taking their children out of the only established church in America, the government school system. Those who are making the crucial stand are those who take this step. It is this step, institutionally speaking, which is separating, not the sheep from the goats, but the shepherds of the future from the about-to-be sheared flocks who will not follow them.

There are many arguments against pulling your children out of the camp of the enemy, and I have heard all of them. But they all boil down to this: Christian schools really don't make that much difference.

As far as the actual schools go, today, it may be true that the secularization of the schools is considerable, even when they are supposedly Christian. What do we expect? We require pastors to attend accredited colleges in order to be ordained; we require college teachers in Christian schools to attend statist, secular universities in order to get their academic degrees; and we require our day school teachers to be certified by some humanist-certified, Ph.D.-holding instructor (or worse, a whole committee of them). We use cast-off State textbooks in the schools. And then we complain because the Christian schools really don't seem so very different from government schools.

One thing is wrong with this argument, at least. At the very least, *we* are financing our own schools, and with financing comes authority. Authority possessed is authority to be used. We can change our Christian schools. We cannot change the government schools, so there is no hope there. Protestants who wouldn't think of spending time and effort to convert Notre Dame University to Protestantism spend lots of time trying to take over a far more secular, government-financed public school system. It makes no sense. At least there is hope for Christian schools. We must labor where there is hope.

CURRICULA Here is where the fight must be made. Here is where our dollars must go. Here is where little is being done. The minds who produce the school curricula for the next generation of Christian youth will provide what has been missing for so long: an integrated program, an intellectual strategy. But to meet a market, these materials must reflect the Christian contributions of many ecclesiastical traditions. We do not have enough potential buyers today to finance a narrow, denominational type of curriculum. Not those of us, at least, who are in churches that did not long ago abdicate by allowing secular humanists to write the denominational school textbooks.

The broad Christian tradition, which is our alternative to humanism, will provide much material for battling the common enemy. The crying need for good, conservative, accurate, principled, readable, and literate curricula will cover many minor disagreements. If love covers a multitude of sins, think what the need for Christian textbooks will cover. And to get the costs down, we have to write for a broad market.

We have a broad position to defend—a position which must be separated from the dying culture of secular humanism. Yet at the same time, we have diverse strands in this Christian tradition, unique elements provided by many Christian groups. We are offering a dying culture a rival, comprehensive culture, meaning a culture broad enough to conquer every nook and cranny on earth. No single ecclesiastical tradition can provide everything needed to replace the humanist system which is disintegrating before our eyes.

Therefore, the Christian school, and the economics of the marketplace, provide the goal and the means of co-operating. Christians cannot afford to be too exclusive today. We simply don't have the funds to be hyper-exclusive. We also don't have the bodies. Like the chaplaincy, we have to put up with diverse ecclesiastical traditions precisely because we are at war, we expect to win, and we cannot ignore help where it is offered.

Now, for those who do not think they are at war, who would not expect to win if they did understand it, and who cannot distinguish a Christian day school from a government day school, all of this may appear silly. After all, they think they have to defend their total institutional purity on questions of dress, drink, prayer, architecture, flip-around collars, or whatever. That's what really counts before God. And if it means shoving the next generation into the training camps of secular humanism, well, then, that's what's necessary. After all, not many people can finance both their ecclesiastical quirks and simultaneously gain full market support for a comprehensive Christian school program. And even among those denominations that have built up their schools, their textbooks have a distressing tendency to resemble secular humanist tracts —baptized by the proper mode, of course.

CONCLUSION Those parents who care enough to get their children into their—the parents'—schools, by financing those schools, will not be so ready to swallow secular humanism, whether presented by men with the proper vestments or not. They are paying for the future, and their vision concerns the future.

The man who sends his children into the public school system is present-oriented, no matter how much he protests. The war against the enemy of Christ, secular humanism, will not be won through the leadership provided by present-oriented defenders of the government school system. The battle for Christian reconstruction is many-faceted, but there is a single "litmus test" to separate the shepherds from the soon-to-be-sheared sheep in this battle: their support—financial, familistic, and verbal—of the Christian day school movement. Anyone who fails this test may still be a regenerate sheep, but he should be recognized as one about to be sheared. If you choose to lead men away from humanism's shearing, rather than follow the flock into the shearing room, then start doing something to build up an independent Christian school, even if the headmaster wears funny collars or no collar at all. And if you can't put up with that, then start your own. But stay out of the camp of the soon-to-be-sheared.

16

THE THREE LEGS OF CHRISTIAN RECONSTRUCTION'S STOOL

"It is clear from church history that each Christian group has made uniquely valuable contributions to the development of the kingdom of God."

One of the most fundamental principles of economics is the division of labor. Adam Smith's opening lines of *The Wealth of Nations* (1776) describes the tremendous increase in productivity which is made possible by the division of labor. He gave his classic example of pin-making. A common laborer could scarcely produce a single pin with a day's labor if he had no specialized pin-making machinery. By breaking up the production of pins into specialized subroutines, ten men in Smith's day were capable of producing 48,000 pins per day, or 4,800 per worker.

Who could afford to buy pins if it took a man a day's labor to produce only one? Not many of us. Yet anyone in England could afford pins in Smith's day, and today they are even cheaper. The wonders of mass production, price competition, specialization of production, and capital equipment have opened a world of productivity and therefore per capita wealth that would have been unattainable by kings as little as two centuries ago—back when there were still kings. We have lost our kings and have gained a kingdom in which almost anyone in industrial nations has more tools and comforts than the kings of the eighteenth century—better medical care (with safe and effective anesthetics), warmer homes in the winter, cooler homes in the summer, and cheaper entertainment every night of the week. What common workman today, lying in a hospital, would voluntarily trade places with anyone on earth living a century ago who was suffering from the same malady?

From whence came the division of labor? From the curse of the ground by God (Gen. 3:17-19) and from the variations in the earth's material resources (including climates) and in human skills and tastes. The curse of the ground is also a blessing: an incentive for men to co-operate with each other in production in order to increase their own personal productivity and therefore their wealth. The productivity which stems from the division of labor places a high price on murder, mayhem, and antisocial behavior. To murder another person is to remove that person's productive contributions from the economy.

ECCLESIASTICAL SPECIALIZATION It is clear from church history that each Christian group has made uniquely valuable contributions to the development of the kingdom of God. Like individuals who specialize, churches also develop skills and resources that increase the productivity of other Christian groups, and society in general. Of course, each group has its own specific weaknesses and vulnerabilities. As conditions change, one or another of these church traditions becomes preeminent, while others fade into the historical shadows. The culture-transforming Catholicism of Augustine in the fifth century became the barren Augustinianism which burdened Luther and led to his challenge to the foundations of Catholic civilization. The dynamic Puritanism of Governor John Winthrop's Massachusetts Bay Colony degenerated into the stodgy, rationalistic, and almost mechanical Calvinism of the early eighteenth century, when it was uprooted by a combination of forces: the Calvinist and pietistic sermons of Jonathan Edwards, the rise of the itinerant Arminian preachers, the liberal Protestantism of Charles Chauncy and other respectable Bostonians, and the mass meetings of Calvinist Anglican George Whitefield. In short, God allows no church tradition to dominate His kingdom after it has atrophied into disuse.

It has become increasingly obvious to serious Christians in our day that the *churches are weak*. They no longer are the primary sources of vision, education, philanthropy, and social cohesion. They no longer exercise a major leadership role nationally, and very little role locally. Fundamentalist churches went into a 50-year cultural retreat after the Scopes' trial in 1925 and after the failure of Prohibition. The liberal denominations have lost their influence markedly since the 1960's. Roman Catholicism has been rent asunder by a series of extraordinary changes that began theologically in the early 1950's ("higher criticism") and institutionally with Pope John XXIII's call for church reform.

But another series of events have begun to rally Christians, luring them back into the arenas of cultural and political conflict. Thousands of fundamentalists have been intellectually encouraged by the publication of anti-evolutionary books and materials since the early 1960's. The legalization of abortion on demand by the U.S. Supreme Court in *Roe v. Wade* (1973) has given Christians of many denominational traditions a cause, and groups are co-operating on an ad hoc basis in order to bring an end to the slaughter of the innocents. The cause of human life has transcended theological disputes that once made co-operation improbable.

As Christians have begun to recognize the religious impulse of modern humanism, they have seen that there are battle lines drawn between the kingdom of God and the kingdom of Satan—battle lines that affect every area of life. The reigning philosophy of neutrality has at last been challenged by Christian leaders (as Marxists challenged it a century ago and philosophical relativists challenged it two generations ago). The implications of this newfound, Bible-based presuppositionalism are becoming clearer to a growing minority of thinking Christians. The intellectual compromises with humanism that once were taken for granted are today being challenged. And as the real threat to Christian civilization is recognized, the former divisions with other Christian groups are being seen as matters of subsidiary importance at this stage of history.

THE NEW CO-OPERATION The rise of the "New Christian Right" in the U.S. since the late 1970's has yet to be fully understood, even by those within the movement. But this much is clear: the increasing arrogance of the humanist elite which controls the West is creating an opposition movement which is itself increasingly confident in the foundations of its own power, namely, the God of the Bible and the power of biblical revelation. Christian leaders who a decade ago would have rejected both doctrines are today preaching about the sovereignty of God and the law of God. A new Puritanism is developing—a Puritanism which offers men the hope of God-honoring social transformation.

This new co-operation can be compared to a stool which rests on three legs. Each leg is important, yet as recently as 1959 these three legs either did not exist or were not being used outside of some narrow denominational tradition. The three legs are: 1) Presbyterian scholarship and six-day creationism; 2) Baptist day schools; and 3) the Pentecostals' various satellite communications systems.

PRESBYTERIAN SCHOLARSHIP Conservative biblical scholarship, outside of the six-day creationism issue and Wycliffe-based linguistic scholarship, has overwhelmingly been Presbyterian in this century. The Lutherans are in second place. This has been true since the 1500's. J. Gresham Machen was fundamentalism's spokesman from 1923 until his death in early 1937, defending biblical inerrancy and attacking theological liberalism, yet Machen was not a fundamentalist. He was a Presbyterian. Even the eloquent William Jennings Bryan was a Presbyterian, although more of a fundamentalist than Machen was. Presbyterian Oswald T. Allis' defense of inerrancy in *God Spake By Moses* was as respected by fundamentalist educators as his critique of dispensationalism was rejected (*Prophecy and the Church*). Francis Schaeffer's influence is obvious—another Calvinistic Presbyterian. R. J. Rushdoony's defense of Christian education (*Intellectual Schizophrenia*) and his critique of humanist education (*The Messianic Character of American Education*) have become "testaments" of the independent Christian education movement in the U.S. His testimony in court trial after court trial as the expert witness for the defense of Christian schools has made him prominent within Baptist and fundamentalist circles. Some Arminian Baptists have even complained publicly about his prominence, but they cannot find anyone with his education and eloquence to fill the gap. They have to put up with him because they have no alternative. In a war, you need to be concerned about how well your partner shoots, not what he believes about the predestined guidance for his bullets.

In short, Presbyterians supply the ammo. They shoot, too, but there just aren't enough of them to make much difference in the front lines.

The confidence provided to modern fundamentalism since 1960 by the various creationist research groups has been crucial. The "shame" of the Scopes' debacle has been cleansed away. The evolutionists are on the run intellectually today, not the creationists. The psychology has shifted from retreat to victory.

BAPTIST DAY SCHOOLS The advent of the Accelerated Christian Education (A.C.E.) program and the Beka Books of the Pensacola Christian School have produced thousands of new independent Christian day schools and church schools since 1965. These schools are molding the minds of the next generation of Christian leaders. They are the knife at the throat of the monopolistic humanist schools, and the humanists know it. The one established church in the U.S., the public school system, is facing the defection of millions of students.

When a parent pulls his child out of a public school and keeps him out *through high school*, he has broken institutionally and psychologically with the statist order. The church that sets up such a school has broadened its commitment to social change. It has also gained an institution which is worth defending, and the humanists are increasingly ready to attack. Thus, the psychology of conformism and capitulation is frequently changed. Pastors who were previously unwilling to make a stand against humanism's myth of neutrality now must make a break. Their schools need a reason to exist. The war against humanism is that reason. Their schools give formerly pietistic pastors the motivation to fight. The pressure from the state boards of education and local truancy officers provides the fight.

PENTECOSTAL SATELLITES The holy rollers are rolling less and broadcasting more than anyone could have guessed a decade ago. A technological miracle is with us, and the Pentecostals are alone making good use of it.

On any given day, 17 commercial broadcasting satellites hang suspended in stationary orbits 23,000 miles above North America. Each satellite offers 24 separate T.V. broadcast channels. Some also offer FM radio. The majority of these channels have no regularly scheduled programming. Thus, they are cheap to rent, and more than other churches, Pentecostal churches are renting them.

A good example is Dr. Gene Scott of the Faith Center in Glendale, California. He had his UHF broadcasting license revoked by the FCC in 1983. Scott was not deterred. He now broadcasts from the Westar Satellite #5 on transponder 1X. He began selling satellite reception dishes that are tuned only to his channel for the incredible price of $777.77. (The average dish sells for over $1,500; they sold for $3,000 when he began his program.) He is making a "technological end run" around the establishment broadcasting media. If Gene Scott can do it, others will do it. The costs of telecommunication are dropping, and this is to the benefit of non-establishment broadcasters.

The potential for education is stupendous. I've

outlined my proposal to revolutionize Christian higher education in my essay, "Levers, Fulcrums, and Hornets" in *Christianity and Civilization*, a symposium on "Tactics of Christian Resistance," which your local bookstore can order from the Geneva Divinty School, Tyler, Texas.

Pastor Robert Tilton of the Word of Faith Church in Dallas has over 1,800 churches hooked up by satellite to his ministry. This is going on unnoticed right under the noses of the humanist elite. He is in a position to reach hundreds of thousands of Christians with a message or even a mobilization effort within a matter of days. (Address for information: P.O. Box 819000, Dallas, TX 75381.)

Thus, the technology is now available for nationwide mobilization for Christian reconstruction. It is cheap enough to be within the grasp of many groups. If Full Gospel Businessmen's Fellowship, the people at *New Wine* magazine, and Maranatha campus ministries ever get their own scheduled satellite broadcasts, the technological foundation of a comprehensive revival will be established.

CONCLUSION We are now in a position to fuse together in a working activist movement the three major legs of the Reconstructionist movement: the Presbyterian-oriented educators, the Baptist school headmasters and pastors, and the charismatic telecommunications system. When this takes place, the whole shape of American religious life will be transformed.

17

CRISIS MANAGEMENT AND FUNCTIONAL ILLITERACY

"The pay-off is the ability to make accurate connections between what the Bible says and the events in the world around us."

The capital asset which is most highly valued in the Bible is godly wisdom. The early chapters of the Book of Proverbs are concerned with this topic, but so are many of the Psalms. Wisdom is worth sacrificing for; it is worth giving up present income in order to store up this most crucial of capital assets.

The trouble with accurate knowledge is that it is very expensive, and the more productive a man is, the more expensive it gets. Why should this be? The reason is simple: the most precious original asset a man has is time. He earns other assets, but he begins with time. God gives a man his alloted portion of time, and the man is judged in terms of the success or failure he produces with his time. Redeeming the time is the fundamental Christian occupation. If a man is able to produce a hundred dollars' worth of goods or services per hour, then every hour used for other purposes costs him, and the community, a hundred dollars. If a man can write an article in a day and earn $1,000, and he instead repairs a leaky faucet, which would have cost him $50 to get repaired by a plumber, then he has lost $950 ($1,000 minus $50, excluding tax considerations). This assumes, of course, that he can crank out $1,000 worth of articles every day of the week, and that the lost income cannot be retrieved by writing the same article the next day, a day which would have been otherwise non-productive.

When anyone develops his talents to the point that he has become a productive member of the community, he finds that his "free" time becomes more precious, precisely because it really isn't free. In fact, of anything he owns, his time is no longer free. A child may have relatively free, meaning inexpensive, time on his hands. He hardly knows what to do with all his spare time. But spare time, or spare anything, is an asset that disappears once the possessor finds ways to put it to profitable, income-producing uses. The day a man finds ways to make money from his spare time is the day he no longer has time to spare. Every minute devoted to watching television is a minute's worth of income forfeited.

BUSY ILLITERATES An illiterate is a person who cannot read. What should we call a person who can read but refuses to? I would call him an illiterate, too. The results are pretty much the same, either way.

Today we find businessmen who cannot find the time to read books. They read the *Wall Street Journal's* headlines. They may read a business magazine and the sports pages of a newspaper. They read business reports from their employers, or from a customer. Perhaps they read a financial newsletter or two. But on the whole, they're stuck. If they don't read, they can only grow or advance along proscribed lines. Not surprisingly, they tend to advance along the lines suggested by their reading. *They advance in those areas where they still continue to read.*

The busy man always places a high premium on his time. Why not? This is his one non-renewable resource. Once an hour is gone, it's gone forever. So the busy man husbands his time. (Some wives believe that the verb, "to husband," when connected to the noun, "time," means "to take away from wives and give to the National Football League.") He allocates it carefully. He doesn't have any time to waste. Time is money. Wasted time is forfeited money. At some point, he is more willing to waste money than time. He pays retail when, with some extra shopping time, he might have paid only wholesale. He isn't being irrational, either. He selects the resource which is less valuable to him, and he is more careless with the less valuable resource.

PASTORAL SCHEDULES What about pastors? They seldom have extra money. At the same time, they seldom have extra time. The pastor, unlike almost all other professionals, is perpetually short of both time and money, from the beginning of his career to the end. He seldom gets ahead on either resource. This is the nature of pastoral service. The pastor may be laying up treasures in heaven, but he is usually devoid of treasures on earth.

The problem the pastor faces is that it is very difficult for him to put a *price tag on his time*. His alternative uses for his time are all non-profit. He doesn't ask himself, "How much money will I lose if I take a day off?" He asks himself, "What services will I not be able to perform if I take a day off?" He can't put a dollar value on his time, precisely because the kinds of services he provides are not normally for sale in a competitive, profit-seeking market. We aren't supposed to sell the message of salvation to the highest bidders. Salvation is not a mass-produced item to be sold through mass-marketing techniques, however often certain modern evangelists try to adapt such techniques.

If a man finds it difficult to put a price tag on his time, then he had better figure out another kind of allocation standard. If five conferences want to get a big-name evangelist to appear in one month, and he isn't willing to sell his time to the highest bidders, then he had better have an alternative standard in mind.

The standards tend to become highly personal, since they are not fundamentally monetary. The pastor decides to counsel someone with a family problem rather than someone else with an employment problem. He tends to cater to those who have problems that match his problem-solving talents. Since he is not operating in a market, he has a tendency to ignore free markets, as well as economic theory. He devotes his time to solving personal problems that are not essentially economic problems. He compares Mary Smith's personal needs with Billy Jones' personal needs, and he doesn't use dollars to evaluate these needs. He doesn't say "Mary has an $87.50 problem, while Billy has a $37.25 problem, so I'll sell my time to Mary, since I can ask up to $50.25 more for my counsel." He says, "Mary has an emotional problem, while Billy has an academic problem, and which is the one which needs a solution immediately? And whose problem can I solve most easily?"

Everyone has problems, and people try to get them solved with the least expenditure of resources. The pastor *gives away his time*, officially. Therefore, *he has to allocate it by non-monetary means*. "Yes, Mary, I'll be able to counsel with you next week. No, I'm not available before then. Yes, I know your husband is a boozer. No, I can't come over now. Well, if he's beating you with a hammer, that's different. Maybe I can make it the day after tomorrow. I'll check my schedule with my secretary."

Pastors have a tendency to get caught up in the "finger-in-the-dyke" syndrome. Which crisis seems imminent? Which one has to be treated immediately? They run from crisis to crisis. Managers do this, too, as the management textbooks tell us, but at least managers can put estimated price tags on their decisions. Ministers of the gospel aren't supposed to

operate in terms of price, at least not until they get
on national television.

One thing is sure: *there will be greater demand for a
pastor's time than his supply of time, at zero price.* His time
is a scarce resource. He has to allocate it. And given
the "finger-in-the-dyke" syndrome, he tends to
become a crisis-management man. He acts in terms
of crises. He learns to allocate his time in terms of
the comparative catastrophe method.

LOW PRIORITY On this scale of measurement,
reading has a low priority. Settling family quarrels is
much higher up. Visiting dignitaries rate higher yet.
Counselling oil executives who tithe is still higher on
the list. ("All souls are equal, but some are more
equal than others.") But reading is down there at the
bottom, running neck-and-neck with catechism
classes, paper cup supplies, and the wife's birthday.

Pastors are too often functional illiterates. This
doesn't mean they can't read. It means they *don't*
read anything except the daily newspaper, overdue
bill notices, and articles under two pages long in
Christianity Today. They read only those items aimed
at people who have lost the ability to discipline themselves enough to tackle anything long, serious, complex, or thought-provoking. Only those pastors who
really enjoy ideas, the way that Pentecostals enjoy
"new things," Episcopalians enjoy prayer breakfasts,
and Presbyterians enjoy committees, are willing to
struggle with tough books.

Serious reading, like serious anything, takes
practice—systematic self-discipline on a long-term

basis. What is reading's pay-off in the short run? Not popular sermons, since congregations that haven't been weaned on complex sermons are unhappy with them at first (and possibly forever). Not more personal income, since congregations are paying for immediate pastoral services, such as counselling and raising money from bake sales. *There is no visible pay-off in the short run.* And besides, word has gotten out about deacon Mitchell and the choir director's daughter, and an annotated bibliography on Bonhoeffer isn't going to help much when *this* crisis blows up. Crisis management reigns supreme.

The problem is, people advance along those lines established by their reading habits. (Or maybe they discipline themselves to read in those areas in which they hope to advance.) Pastors who have become busy illiterates are almost guaranteeing their personal stagnation. The best they can hope for is bigger, more influential stagnation, or even syndicated stagnation. ("Keep those cards and letters coming, friends, and be sure to let your local station manager know how much you appreciate these broadcasts.") A program of systematic reading must be started early, maintained continually, and adhered to religiously. If it isn't, crisis management will overcome good intentions and thereby guarantee personal stagnation.

CRISES AND SOLUTIONS It may not be possible to break bad habits without getting an immediate pay-off. If crisis management has become basic to a man's ministry, meaning his allocation of time, then

he may have to start reading in those areas related to
the predominant crisis. It may be marital problems.
It may be personal finances. It may be church finances. It may be problems with certain age groups. It
may be anything, but there are books written constantly to deal with these issues. If it takes crises to
get a man reading systematically, then at least they
have produced positive change in someone.

Crisis management should not become a way of
life for pastors. The pastoral function is more than
beating away wolves. If a pastor makes it clear that
the basis of his ministry is crisis management, then
congregation members who want a piece of the
pastor's time will manufacture a crisis or two. Sheep
in wolves' clothing will become a familiar phenomenon in pastoral counselling.

One way to clear up crises is to identify profit-
seeking professionals in the Christian community,
and then direct crisis-prone church members to these
professionals. There are too many pastors who are
spending too much time holding the hands of people
who really only want someone to complain to, free of
charge. The pastor had better seek out professional
counsellors to whom these people can be sent,
checkbook in hand, after the second session. Or if
this isn't possible, the people needing the counselling
had better be shown how much benefit personal
sacrifice would be. Let them learn to work. Like the
dried-out rummies in Alcoholics Anonymous, these
people need to find someone even worse off than
they are to go and help. Pastors have to stop
operating the local Institute for the Absorption of

Pastoral Time. They have to get people thinking in terms of costs. They have to find ways to put price tags on their services, if only to cut down the demand. Let time-absorbing people donate money to the church. Maybe pastors can't legitimately make a profit this way, but they can at least reduce demand. If someone has to pay in order to solve a problem, he will tend to get the problem solved faster. He will cooperate with the problem-solver, not return with ever-new problems for the solver to deal with, free of charge. He will accept a solution sooner.

NO DIPLOMAS Students will read systematically in order to earn a diploma. There is a great temptation to stop reading and learning, once there is no one remaining who will offer still another diploma, or no one who cares whether anyone holds one.

The pay-off for the pastor isn't another diploma. The pay-off is the ability to make accurate connections between what the Bible says and the events in the world around us. We are to exercise dominion. Books open up the areas subject to biblical dominion. The pastor who does not read will not be ready to call all men to the tasks of dominion. Stagnation isn't the proper goal. The computer boys tell us, concerning inaccurate data, "garbage in, garbage out." The pastor's version is, "pabulum in, pabulum out." Used pabulum isn't going to turn the world around.

18

PASTORAL EDUCATION

"If you are not sufficiently self-disciplined to get your education this way, you are probably not ready to become a full-fledged 'theological revolutionary' at this stage of your career."

From time to time, I receive letters from young pastors or men thinking of going into the ministry. They say something like this: "I have read your books and the books and newsletters published by people in the 'Christian reconstruction' movement. I want to further my education in this area. Where do you recommend that I go to school, and what subjects should I study?"

This sort of letter is heartening and disheartening. It is heartening because those of us who do a lot of writing always like to know that there are people out there who are reading our materials. Even more important, they are absorbing what we say, and are now thinking about devoting years of study to rethinking a particular academic discipline or other area of dominion. This is the sort of response that shows us that what we are saying is getting through.

Yet such a letter is also disheartening. It points out to us in all clarity just how few institutional structures are ready to impart the kind of message we are presenting. Young men who run across our materials have stumbled into "the hard corps." They may not yet grasp the implications of just how early they have arrived at the "party."

I haven't ever read that Marx and Engels received letters from enthusiastic new converts asking to be directed in their graduate studies. I never read anything about Marx and Engels setting up some sort of accredited Communist training program. The same holds true of Charles Darwin, as far as I'm aware. But if such letters had come, what could the founders of these enormously successful ideological movements have said in the year, say, 1862?

First, the movements were new. They were essentially armchair revolutions. Marx and Engels wrote books, pamphlets, newspaper articles, endless numbers of letters, and monographs. They wrote, between them, from the early 1840's until the 1890's. The quantity of their materials is huge. Much of the correspondence is still untranslated. Between them, they reshaped the thinking of several generations of revolutionaries and socialists. But they never started a university. They never even published a newsletter. (Inconceivable!)

Darwin is known for his two major works on evolution, *Origin of Species* (note: no "the") and *Descent of Man.* He wrote many other books on flowers, animals, and other detailed and long-forgotten topics. He carried on a voluminous correspondence. But as a semi-invalid, he never organized a meeting or started a graduate school program. He sat on his couch and watched the plants move. (Literally, that's what he did, months on end.) Then he wrote up his observations. He changed the world.

EARLY PHASES When a new ideological or religious movement appears, it generally is marked by several features: little money, few followers, lots of opposition, little if any co-operation from existing institutions, young followers, experimentation, dead ends, and an emphasis on communications. Sometimes the communications system is verbal, meaning face to face. Sometimes it is written: pamphlets, books, newsletters, etc. But the message is the key for long-term results; no "charismatic" prophet can supervise the movement after he is dead. For the movement to survive, it requires a body of written material (unless it is strictly "hermetic," meaning initiatory, occult, and elitist).

The problem which faces the adherents of a new movement—religious, scientific, ideological, political—is that its unique perspective condemns it in the eyes of those who have established the existing institutions. Worse: those who work within the "nearest" institutions to the new one—meaning the closest ideologically or philosophically—are those who are most likely to resist the spread of the "new doctrine." The proponents of the "new doctrine" (or new applications of the older, established doctrine) are saying, in effect: "Those who have gone before did not see the full implications. Their successors have clung for too long to outmoded views, repeating the words of the Founders. It is time to examine and apply the implications of the older view." In short, the newcomers are calling into question the vision, or integrity, or competence of all their "ideological first cousins." They are telling the world (meaning a handful of people who will listen) that the people who are defenders of the "received faith" are no longer able to apply the underlying implications of the received faith to modern conditions. Thus, the directors of the existing institutions will do what is necessary to see to it that proponents of the new vision are kept far away from the seats of institutional power. The newcomers are regarded as a greater intellectual threat than the "unbelievers outside the camp."

The younger men, or newly converted believers from "outside the camp," who respond favorably to the explanations of the new perspective will be interested in furthering their education. But they almost invariably make a fundamental mistake. They assume that educational techniques are essentially the same everywhere: old movement, new movement, and partially accepted movement. Not so. Educational techniques vary considerably, depending on which phase of the movement we are dealing with.

In the early phase, there are many loose ends. A comprehensive system has not yet been developed.

The strength of the newer outlook is not found in its comprehensive system; it is found in its vision, its ability to provide better answers for old questions that were never answered very well, and answers for new questions that the establishment has refused to answer at all. But the new movement possesses no "bricks and mortar" to speak of. It has no university. It offers no certification.

Certification comes after conquest. Then the victors begin to certify the recruits. But this is long after the older "establishment" scholars have retired, died, or in rare instances, converted over to the newer viewpoint. Education then becomes far more institutionalized and ritualized. The teachers become more conventional, less innovative, more patient diggers in the garden. They synthesize, popularize, summarize, and make acceptable the ideas that were anathema a decade or millennium earlier. "The owl of Minerva flies only at dusk," Marx used to say: the final synthesis of a culture's underpinnings comes only at the end of that culture.

So in the early phase of a movement, the students must be educated "in the field" or "on the job." They must learn to read voluminously, widely, and even wildly. They have to start asking themselves such questions as: "How are these questions answered by today's establishment representatives?" "What is the more likely way to approach this question, given the perspective of the new view?" "Where can I find out the sources of information I need to begin to create new answers?" "What questions simply cannot be dealt with successfully by today's conventional approaches?" By looking at the established body of opinion from a new perspective, the newcomer discovers better ways to answer perplexing questions.

Still, if he is beguiled by the educational techniques of the older, established instructors, he becomes confused. He wants the *new, improved version* from an *old, established institution.* But this is possible only by seeking out a few "closet revolutionary" scholars who hold to the new views, men who will be oddballs within their own niche of the education system. The student is faced with being the oddball's boy. His only alternative is to become a closet revolutionary student until his degree is in hand and the academic exercises are over. The student doesn't reveal the details of his faith while he is running the academic gauntlet.

SELF-EDUCATION The best way to get educated in the early phases of a movement is to sit down and read every book, document, and pamphlet produced by members of the movement. The reader has to think through the new material, integrate it with what he has believed in the past, and sort it out for himself. Few people are ever trained to work this way, but it must be done. Only a few people will follow through, which is why new ideological movements are initially made up of a remnant.

The typical approach to education is to have a reading list (not too long), assigned to a person, which is then followed by a series of boiled-down lectures, interspersed with exercises known as examinations. The material is "packaged" in a format which would be familiar to someone who went to school half a millennium ago. Such an educational program is suited for the middle and final stages of a world-and-life view. It is not suitable for the early phases of a so-called "paradigm shift." (The phrase appears in the important book by Thomas Kuhn, *The Structure of Scientific Revolutions*, University of Chicago Press, 2nd edition, 1970.)

The textbook is familiar to every student. Generally conventional, unmemorable, carefully organized, and frequently revised, the textbook is a compilation of the accepted interpretations of an era. Textbooks are written for comparatively large audiences of complacent students, who are cramming their heads full of new (to them) information in preparation for an exam. Textbooks are seldom written to offer a totally new world-and-life view. A revolutionary book necessarily has a limited audience, since few if any educational institutions will adopt it for use in the classroom.

Textbooks are written in order to restructure facts in terms of a perspective. It takes time to recruit and train people who can write textbooks. Innovators are seldom skilled popularizers. Furthermore, they are too busy rethinking bits and pieces of the known world in terms of their new perspective. Big chunks of the "accepted wisdom" remain untouched by the innovation for decades. Thus, textbooks produced by representatives of a new view tend to be uneven: revolutionary in some sections, conventional in others. It takes years of rethinking and recruiting to develop textbook writers.

The desire of students to have a packaged educational program dropped into their laps, with a conventionally structured program of lectures, exams, and certification, cannot be fulfilled in the early phases of a movement. Students who are attracted to some new perspective may resent having to learn everything twice—once in a conventional classroom and again on their own—but they have no option. They cannot get what they want, namely, a spoon-fed education of the revolutionary material within the standard educational framework.

Self-education is the necessary approach. Material learned in the classroom must be unlearned in the library. The institutional bases of the two movements are different. The establishment has bricks and mortar, conventional instruction, uninspired teaching, scholarship money, certification, and continual intellectual reinforcement. The revolutionaries have a compelling vision, innovative books, little money for scholarships, no certification, and a willingness to probe "banned" topics or discussion.

CONCLUSION Probably the best way for a student to get a revolutionary education in a conventional world is to attend a school where students are presumed to be competent and independently motivated. Such schools allow far more freedom to students to select topics and educational programs on their own. Better a British or Scottish university than an American state university; better a graduate school program than an undergraduate one.

The other approach is to locate a closet revolution-

ary instructor at some universtiy and go to study with
him, and (if possible) with him alone. Become an apprentice. Forget about graduating, unless it takes little extra time and work. Just learn the material.

A reading list designed by a representative of the
new perspective is the best way to achieve the education that will pay off. Reading 50 relevant books and
thinking about them beats almost any spoon-feeding
program that a conventional school can provide.

The fact is, unconventional people must pioneer
unconventional perspectives. The search for a conventional academic program to attain unconventional material is close to self-defeating. It expects
too much from established institutions. The person
who thinks he needs a conventional academic setting
in order to achieve full status as a revolutionary had
better wait for 30 or 50 years, until the new perspective has demonstrated its power by picking off one or
two conventional institutions. By then the new
perspective will have become sufficiently conventional and watered down to make it acceptable.

My advice: save your tuition money. Get a job.
Read in your spare time. If you are determined to
continue your formal education, sign up for the introductory correspondence course in theology from
Geneva Divinity School, 708 Hamvasy, Tyler, Texas
75701. Complete the course and take another. If you
are not sufficiently self-disciplined to get your education this way, you probably are not ready to become
a full-fledged "theological revolutionary" at this stage
of your career.

If you want a conventional program, think about

St. Andrews University in Scotland, or the University of Manchester, or some other British university. Go in, write your thesis, take your orals, and graduate. Get finished as fast as possible. If you think you need to go to seminary, think again; anyone who needs a conventional seminary education probably shouldn't be contemplating the ministry anyway. Better to apprentice with a master church-builder or Christian counsellor, and learn directly.

19

REVIVING APPRENTICESHIP

"... it is mandatory that a person who possesses certain skills reach back and pull along another person who is farther behind; this is how improvements in everyone's productivity and income are increased."

Several years ago, I visited the apartment of Swami Kriyanada (Donald Walters), the author of *The Path: Autobiography of a Western Yogi*. He is a follower of Paramahansa Yogananda, the founder of the Self-Realization Fellowship, an organization devoted to bringing Eastern and Western thought together. Mr. Walters subscribed at that time to the *Ruff Times*, and he was very interested in survivalism — a 3-G's program of God, gold, and groceries (but no guns). I spoke at his Ananda Center — near Grass Valley, California — a communal community, but without shared wives or compulsory socialism. Several members are successful small businessmen, and their businesses seem to be respected in the nearby community. I gave my speech on the four stages of the tax revolt, and the response was as enthusiastic as any I have received on the "hard money" lecture circuit.

One of the features of most communes which is almost universal is the presence of some sort of apprenticeship program. These communes are convinced that basic skills must be imparted from experienced workers to the inexperienced, not in the classroom, but on the job. The Ananda Fellowship has a very sophisticated print shop that enables them to produce paperback books by the tens of thousands.

Walters showed me the most remarkable table and chair set that I have ever seen. It was carved by an aging craftsman in India who sold it to him for, as I remember, about $2,000. The carvings were so intricate that it was like looking at a medieval cathedral or some other major work of art. You simply cannot buy a new piece of furniture like this any longer.

The craftsman knew it would be the last representative of a very special art form. Walters told me what the old man had told him: "I cannot get apprentices any longer to carry on the tradition. Anyone with half the skills needed to produce this would be highly employable at far more money in a conventional furniture business. In fact, to get the carvings just right, the muscle and bone structure of the arm and wrist must be developed before the boy is 12 years old; if he has not begun his apprenticeship much earlier, he will never develop the skill. I am the last of those who can produce such works."

The old man may have been exaggerating, but when a master craftsman tells me that such and such is basic to his craft, I am not in a position to argue. Perhaps a physiologist might object. Certainly, the manipulation skills—the "feel" for the use of the tools—must have been limited to those who had experienced long years of training.

During my speech, I discussed my theory that it is mandatory that a person who possesses certain skills reach back and pull along another person who is farther behind; this is how improvements in everyone's productivity and income are increased. I mentioned an old recommendation I read in a book on management that no one should be promoted in a company until he has trained two men who can replace him. Afterwards, one of the members told me that Walters' philosophy is that each man needs to train seven potential replacements.

WHY APPRENTICESHIP? It is odd that two men, operating with such different theological and philosophical presuppositions as Walters and I hold, should be in such agreement about the educational process. The impersonalism of bureaucracy, especially educational bureaucracy, repels us both. We are convinced that the best managers are trained by successful managers, and that personal contact with craftsmen, on the job, provides more insight into the actual workings of the world than a detailed textbook explanation.

The "personal touch" is a real phenomenon. If we

had to explain verbally every decision, meaning every factor involved in a decision, we would forever be explaining, never producing. There are aspects of any production process that cannot be put into words effectively. The worker has to get a "feel" for the overall process. Thus the kind of training imparted by formal education has definite limits.

Another factor which cannot be comprehensively described or put into predictable formulas is entrepreneurship. The nature of entrepreneurship is essentially non-rational, if by "rational" we mean abstract and calculable. Entrepreneurs must forecast future market conditions and then organize the production process to meet the needs of that future market. If a computer could do it, there would be neither profit nor loss in an economy. Teaching entrepreneurship by means of a textbook is not possible; what a textbook can teach is that which is *not* entrepreneurship — mathematically calculable risks, measurement techniques, cause-and-effect events, data processing. This reduces the range of the unknown, thereby transferring the responsibility of dealing with these issues from entrepreneurship to management. Entrepreneurs then use new, "hard" data to make judgments concerning the economic future. But these techniques are not the heart of entrepreneurship, any more than knowledge of a batter's hitting percentage is the heart of being a major league baseball pitcher. (Can you imagine a baseball team that would hire its pitchers on the basis of their scores on computerized examinations on physiology, aerodynamics, and batter's statistics?)

There is a tendency for educated men to discount

the knowledge possessed by skilled illiterates. Economist Thomas Sowell has stated it well: "Although the phrase 'ignorant savage' may be virtually self-contradictory, it is a common conception, and one with a certain basis. The savage is wholly lacking in a narrowly specific kind of knowledge: abstract, systematized knowledge of the sort generally taught in schools. Considering the enormous range of human knowledge, from intimate personal knowledge of specific individuals to the complexities of organizations and the subtleties of feelings, it is remarkable that one speck in this firmament should be the sole determinant of whether someone is considered knowledgeable or ignorant *in general*. Yet it is a fact of life that an unlettered peasant is considered ignorant, however much he may know about nature and man, and a Ph.D. is never considered ignorant, however barren his mind might be outside his narrow specialty and however little he grasps about human feelings or social complexities." (*Knowledge and Decisions* [New York: Basic Books, 1980], p. 8.)

It is obvious that the training which is considered basic for the pastorate is the training of the seminary classroom, which is essentially bureaucratic and rationalistic. The Bible, in contrast, describes the criteria of the eldership as being essentially personal and familistic (I Tim. 3:1-7). The same is true of the office of deacon (I Tim. 3:8-13). Protestants, especially the more "magisterial" Protestants — Presbyterians, Anglicans, and Lutherans — have stressed academic performance over apprenticeship. The result has been the capture of the denominations by liberals, who first captured the classrooms which the prospective pastors have been required to attend. The most conservative churches are usually those whose pastors have not been required to submit themselves to the gauntlet of higher formal eduation.

MARKET PERFORMANCE Every organization has criteria of performance. Bureaucracies have formal rules and regulations that must be adhered to. Profit management firms have the criterion of profit. The formal rules and regulations are means to an end: *profit*. There is an independent standard of performance. Bureaucratic management has no comparable independent performance standard.

Colleges and universities tend to produce people who are trained to perform bureaucratically: tests, term papers, and other formal criteria. Graduates tend to want to pursue life formally, since they have demonstrated their capacity to take examinations. As one very successful taker of computerized tests once told me, "I would like to find a job where I would be required only to take tests, since that is the one skill I have picked up in college." Problem: no private, profit-seeking firm rewards employees primarily for passing exams, once they have actually been hired. Performance on the job is far more crucial. Buyers care nothing about the formal structure of the corporation; what they are buying is a final product.

To maintain profits in a shifting market, firms must maintain flexibility. Unlike subsidized bureaucracies, profit-seeking firms must deal with the shifting demands of customers. The same is true of churches: they cannot be operated as if they were seminaries. If they are managed in this way, they will perish.

CHURCH APPRENTICESHIP TRAINING Every church should begin a program that will bring together skilled older working men and younger men who need guidance and training. When men with craft skills or business skills are not training apprentices, their talents are not being put to maximum use. Churches need a balanced membership. A church with no members except dentists or lawyers would be dismal. A church composed primarily of college graduates is also handicapped.

There is a tendency to push young people into college. This increases the number of those who are subjected to bureaucratic thinking and training. It narrows the church's membership base.

The Puritans of New England used to send their children to be apprentices at young ages: under 10 years old. They wanted to secure for their children on-the-job training by independent judges of their skills. Modern parents have few similar options. The church today is in a position to encourage successful older members to take on apprentices from the church. If they receive no salary, apprentices are not subject to minimum wage laws. It is illegal to work for a dollar an hour or a penny an hour; it is not illegal to work for free.

Modern minimum wage laws are designed to keep young people out of the work force. This is a subsidy to trade union members, who now face less competition from price-competitive younger workers who are being partially subsidized by their parents (room and board, etc.), and who can therefore work for less. By establishing apprenticeship programs, churches could escape this key restriction on the development of talent.

Another possible area of church service would be the recruiting of minority youths from local minority group churches. Minimum wage laws are especially oppressive to minority youths. Teenagers are effectively locked out of the legal job markets. They do not develop the necessary psychological and technical skills to become effective employees. The public schools ruin them academically, while minimum wage laws ruin them entrepreneurially. They can deal in drugs, steal cars, or go into petty crime, for older entrepreneurs in these fields are happy to provide them with training and minimal capital. They can receive on-the-job training from criminals who care nothing about minimum wage laws. In ccontrast, law-abiding youths find themselves unable to attach themselves to entrepreneurs. They cannot legally receive training from profit-seeking local businessmen.

The result of minimum wage laws has been the increasing reliance of minority populations on the welfare State and its endless bureaucratic rules and regulations. Their brightest students go into the professions (monopolies protected from price competition), the government, teaching, bureaucratic corporations seeking to comply with "equal employment" rules, and crime. No tradition of small business can develop, as it has in oriental and Jewish neighborhoods that have family businesses that are exempt from minimum wage restrictions regarding young family members.

The "generation gap" is made wider by separating potential apprentices from potential masters. The needs of each group for the talents of the other cannot be fulfilled legally through employment contracts. The public schools, with their bureaucratic regimentation, their poorly paid humanist faculties, their lack of on-the-job training, and their confiscated tax revenues, are not turning out dedicated, skilled entrepreneurs. They reproduce their own kind: bureaucrats. What else should we expect? Do medical schools produce lawyers? Do law schools produce physicists? Why should we expect bureaucratic institutions to produce entrepreneurs and craftsmen?

CONCLUSIONS The diaconates have a remarkable opportunity. They can help bring together masters and apprentices. They can establish programs that will enable families to obtain the specialized training for children which is almost unavailable through conventional educational institutions. Masters can see their skills and respect for craftsmanship passed along to another generation—a motive shared by masters throughout history. The public schools, in their quest for ever-greater bureaucratic power over society, have nearly destroyed the independent crafts. The church can help to restore the crafts to their former position.

20

BRUSH-FIRE WARS

"... my tactic has a strictly economic goal: to *lower the costs of defending our Constitutional liberties*, on the one hand, and to *raise the costs to the State of infringing upon our Constitutional liberties*, on the other."

The escalation of Federal, state, and local pressure against Christian schools has reached a crisis stage. (The escalation of pressure against churches is in the early stages.) Day after day, headmasters are being put under new bureaucratic regulations. No longer is the battle against Christian schools being left to amateur prosecuting attorneys. The bureaucrats are bringing out their biggest guns.

There are many reasons for this escalation of pressure. The private school movement is now visibly threatening the survival of the modern humanist State's most important institution, the public school. The public school is the humanists' equivalent of the established church. The priesthood of State-certified teachers no longer has its monopoly. The source of new recruits to the humanist State is being reduced drastically. The inner-city schools are already doomed. By 1980, under 27% of the schoolchildren in the Los Angeles city schools were white; four years earlier, the proportion had been about 40%. Forced busing had been ideologically consistent with bureaucratic equalitarianism, but it had also been institutionally suicidal. Only when forced busing ended in the fall of 1984 did white students start leaving the non-public high schools to return to *suburban* public schools in Los Angeles.

Within a decade, the public school systems of the major cities will be overwhelmingly composed of poorly trained, poorly motivated minority students whose academic skills will not be adequately developed by the modernist education methods. The academic standards of the public school products have been falling. From 1963 until 1983, test scores on the Scholastic Aptitude Tests (SAT's) dropped lower.

The cities are desperate. As white middle-class families depart, in order to escape forced busing (forced racial and above all *social* integration), the tax base of the large cities erodes. Parents who have their children in private schools are no longer interested in voting in favor of huge bond issues for the construction of more public schools. Who cares if public school teachers are denied higher salaries? Not the parents of students in private schools. "Let public school teachers go on strike! Let them starve!" The *tax revolt against large-city public schools* is now a reality. The cities are now in a downward spiral. The more liberal ("feed me, house me, clothe me") the voting patterns in the cities, the more the taxpaying, employed citizens flee to the suburbs. They try to escape from the politics of envy. (Gary North, *Successful Investing in an Age of Envy* [2nd ed.; P.O. Box 8204, Ft. Worth, TX: Steadman Press, 1983, $19.95]).

PRIVATE SCHOOLS To stop the spread of private schools, the bureaucrats are creating an endless series of regulations that are designed to raise the costs of private education and thereby reduce the number of students who enroll. The most important tactic is to use judicial harassment. It is expensive for tiny, struggling schools to hire top-flight legal talent. The states, in contrast, are using tax money to send in waves of lawyers to do their best to tie up private schools in red tape and restrictions. How can a small school expect to win? How many well trained, effective lawyers are there who are familiar with the legal issues involved? Not many.

What we need in education is precisely what we need in every other area of life: *decentralization*. We need an army of dedicated Christian school headmasters who are ready to say "no" to the bureaucrats and defend their schools successfully in court. We do not need large national organizations that are easy to infiltrate, buy off, sidetrack, or frighten. Such organizations are run by bureaucrats, not fighters. The bureaucrats of the State see bureaucrats in large private organizations as their allies. But small local schools are driving the bureaucrats crazy. They are springing up everywhere. They do not report on what they are doing or where they are. These schools are like hornets. There are too many of them to fight effectively one by one.

THE LEGAL BATTLE The tactical problem facing Christians is this: How can we gain the benefits of a centralized, well-paid organization, yet avoid the concomitant bureaucratization? How can we mobilize the army, yet keep all the troops in the field, constantly sniping at the enemy? How can we train local men to carry the battle to government officials, yet make certain that the local people are ready and able to fight successful battles? We do not want legal precedents going against us because the local headmasters and their lawyers were not well prepared. We already face a situation where the civil governments are attacking schools continually in order to get adverse legal precedents.

Obviously, few churches and Christian schools can afford to hire local lawyers at $100 per hour. Besides, lawyers face the problem of specialization. They have to educate themselves in a new field. There are cases to read, arguments to master, in state after state. There is no doubt that since the late 1970's, there has been a co-ordinated effort on the part of Federal, state, and local education officials to limit the Christian schools. The state attorneys are no longer being surprised by new arguments of the defense lawyers, as they were in the early 1970's. Precedents are going against Christian schools today. Prosecuting attorneys know who the better-known defense witnesses are and what they will say.

There are no more easily won cases. The enemy is well-armed in this battle. Our people are poorly armed, except when the very best, most prominent defense attorneys have been hired. (The most prominent of these attorneys are not always the best, especially when their tiny organizations are fighting hundreds of cases. Never hire an attorney to fight your case if he has over five potential trial cases in progress. Ask!) There are few of these men to go around. They ask and receive high fees, too, or are forced to raise the money from hard-pressed donors.

Yet the enemy has problems, too. First, the religious traditions of the United States stand against them. So do the legal traditions. Second, there are only so many top-flight prosecuting attorneys. The government lawyers at the local level are not usually "the best and the brightest." If they were really good, they would be in private practice making three times the pay. Third, the State still faces the threat of jury trials, and these juries are sometimes filled with people who are sick and tired of being kicked around by bureaucrats. So the war is not over. Christians and independent school supporters have the principles on their side, and the civil government has both the initiative and the money.

What we need is to take advantage of our greatest strength: *numbers*. We have many schools and churches that need their independence. If we could get the State to commit more men and resources to the fight, we would find that the quality of our opponents would drop. Their best legal talent would be tied up in other court battles.

JAMMED COURTS The court system is becoming vulnerable. Courts are tied up today in a series of endless appeals. (Macklin Fleming, *The Price of Perfect Justice* [New York: Basic Books, 1974]). It is becoming very expensive to prosecute a case successfully these days, which is why defense lawyers are getting reduced sentences or suspended sentences for their clients through plea-bargaining (pleading guilty to lesser crimes). The accused agree to plead guilty to lesser charges rather than tie up the courts in long cases to prove that the accused committed a major crime. So far, Christian pastors and Christian school headmasters have not been willing to play this plea-bargaining game. Therefore, it will tie up more of the State's economic resources if we stand firm. If we do not capitulate, but force the prosecutors to prove every point in court, we can make it very expensive for the civil government to prosecute hundreds of schools. If we can find a way *to reduce our costs of defense*, simultaneously *increasing the costs of prosecution*, we can make the State think twice about initiating new suits against us. How can we do it?

The best way to get most things accomplished is to persuade a skilled worker that he has both principle and a profit potential on his side. Show him how to do well by doing good.

Highly skilled lawyers need good incomes to lure them away from the more lucrative ways to practice law. New lawyers are becoming a glut on the market; they will practice for less money. Is there a way to enlist the services of skilled lawyers for lots of money, *pay them once*, and then use their skills to mobilize lots of lower paid new lawyers to become the *legal shock troops* in a long battle against bureaucratic tyranny?

Here is a list of needed services to defend the Christian school movement: 1) a master lawyer who is skilled in the field of private education law, and who is also 2) skilled in communicating this knowledge to his peers; 3) a series of publications that enable non-lawyers to defend their own cause; 4) a strategy geared to the mobilization of thousands of independent schools; 5) a tactical program which will work at the local level. We need a skilled motivator at the top, and men at the local level willing to fight.

A DEFENSE PACKAGE What if some bright lawyer could offer the following publications package? *First*, an *introductory, inflammatory paperback book* which offers some true "horror stories" of bureaucratic tyranny, and how the defendants successfully defended themselves. This inexpensive, mass-produced book would contain a tear-out sheet for people to order information about a local defense program.

Second, the lawyer would publish a *manual for self-defense*. It would be a "do it yourself" guide for Christian school headmasters: what to do in the preliminary stages. For example, it would teach that most crucial of all responses to inquiries from bureaucrats: **"Write me a letter."** It would contain a series of sample letters which will escalate the intensity of the resistance, letters requesting further information, including the statute by means of which the bureaucrat is taking action, and information on why this statute applies in this instance to the school in question. Letters, letters, and more letters. This is the tactic of *Lawyer Delay*. Meanwhile, the headmaster or pastor can begin to prepare the second phase of the defense. But Lawyer Delay can provide extra time. Make sure the opposition really has a legal case before capitulating to anything, signing anything, agreeing to anything, or paying anything.

The manual would contain "nuts and bolts" information for non-lawyers: how to write letters of inquiry, how to file official protests, what *not* to admit or agree to, where to get procedural help, where to locate defense witnesses, a list of law firms or independent lawyers specializing in school cases, which forms to fill out, where to get them, etc. This would be a *layman's introduction*. Price: around $100.

Third, the master lawyer would produce a *lawyer's defense manual*. It would contain relevant precedents, information on which arguments seem to be working, transcripts of testimony from successful cases, and a history of the legal battle. This would be sold to lawyers directly by the master lawyer, or sold to a Christian school to give to a local lawyer hired by the school. The idea is to save the local lawyer time in looking up the cases. At $100 per hour, the school needs to save the lawyer all the time it can. The idea is to avoid reinventing the wheel at $100 per hour. Price: $100-$200.

Fourth, the master lawyer can supply *updates* to the lawyer's manual. He can keep up with precedents. This new information would become a source of continuing income for him. It would help finance his continuing research in the field.

Fifth, sell a monthly *newsletter*, or raise tax-deductible money with a free one, to alert pastors and headmasters of the problem.

All of these projects could be accomplished through a profit-seeking organization run by the master lawyer. It could also be accomplished through a non-profit legal defense organization. The idea is to get the *benefits of legal specialization* along with the benefits of *decentralized multiple defense initiatives*.

I want to make it perfectly clear that my tactic is not aimed at clogging the courts. Clogging the courts as a tactic is illegal. It is classified as "obstructing justice." People who publicly recommend court-clogging as a tactic can get into trouble with the authorities, just as black people in Montgomery, Alabama, could get in trouble in 1955 for promoting a boycott of the local transit system. In contrast, my tactic has a strictly economic goal: to *lower the costs of defending our Constitutional liberties*, on the one hand, and to *raise the costs to the State of infringing upon our Constitutional liberties*, on the other.

Our goal should be to make it almost prohibitively expensive for bureaucrats to initiate unconstitutional attacks on our little institutions. If we can do this, then the State will begin to reduce its reliance on judicial harassment to drive innocent victims out of existence.

I have a dream, as one former media manipulator once said. I have a dream of fearless Christian school headmasters walking arm-in-arm with fearless laymen, whose legal training has been sufficient to

equal $1,400 worth of legal talent. I have a dream of
avoiding the use of defense lawyers in 60% of the
harassment cases. I have a dream of headmasters being able to hold out until the last minute before having to hire any lawyer, and then paying him as little
as possible to do his preliminary homework. I have a
dream of making it so expensive for prosecuting attorneys to take on a Christian school that they will
spend more of their time prosecuting murderers,
rapists, and burglars, if only because they will spend
less time and achieve greater success, case for case,
than prosecuting Christians. I have a dream of
desperate local education officials, bogged down in a
mountain of paper, trying to figure out how all these
evils came upon them. I have a dream of weary
judges reading defense motions to dismiss, and being driven to distraction by skilled defense lawyers
who follow lawyer William Kunstler's tactic of objec-
ting to everything the prosecution says all day long.
And I have a dream of being able to buy the basic
tools in two manuals for no more than $300.

My dream would be the State's nightmare.

Why is it that no lawyer has produced this sort of
program? I wish I knew. The money is there. The
institutional pay-off is there. It is clear that the
clients will soon be there, if harassment escalates.
Why don't we see Christian school defense manuals,
and anti-abortion tactical manuals, and how to de-
incorporate your church manuals? Why do Christian legal groups feel compelled to do everything "in-
house," and not decentralize the whole Christian
defense system through the use of training manuals?

Have our Christian lawyers adopted the mentality of empire-builders? Have they all decided that if they cannot personally oversee a case from start to finish, that it is better that the victims not be defended? It looks that way.

TAKING THE OFFENSIVE What we desperately need is *decentralization*. We need to take advantage of our numbers. If one church or school is threatened, then every church and school in the region should publicly state that it is doing precisely what the school under attack is doing, and that the authorities had better take them to court, too. Then each group begins a counter-suit under the civil rights statutes. Each church sues the bureaucrat who takes steps to challenge a particular group's civil rights.

We need *brush-fire wars*, all over the country. We need to show the bureaucrats that they cannot stop the spread of the Christian fire by putting out one blaze. They have to put out hundreds of blazes. They cannot do it if enough of us get involved. (I am not suggesting that this tactic will work only if everyone gets involved. No tactic should ever be begun which relies on "getting everyone involved" to achieve success. But the more who start getting involved, the tougher it will be on opponents.)

If you are a headmaster or pastor who would want to buy such a defense package, or if you are a local lawyer who wants to get involved in defending Christian causes, or if you think you are sufficiently skilled to become a master lawyer who will publish such materials, contact the John Whitehead's organization:

Rutherford Institute
P.O. Box 510
Manassas, VA 22110

Until Christians are ready to enlist the support of lawyers in some system of decentralized defense, there is little hope that a systematic, concerted, effective national campaign against local harassment will be launched. When churches begin encouraging one or two members to learn the rudiments of legal research, churches will become less vulnerable to attack. When there are lawyer-directed home study courses in how to become a *Christian paralegal activist*, we will know that a new day has dawned. This may be a decade or more away, but it is eventually going to come.

[For more information, see the book I edited, *Tactics of Christian Resistance*, which your bookstore can order from Geneva Divinity School, 708 Hamvassy, Tyler, Texas 75701.]

21

CHURCH NEWSLETTERS

". . . they are effective because they are read."

As you might imagine, I'm a firm supporter of newsletters. I support myself by means of *Remnant Review*, my economic report. I keep people interested in the Institute for Christian Economics by means of the various letters put out by I.C.E. I have found that my newsletter essays are quoted more widely than my books. So in terms of short-run impact, the newsletter is a better medium than books.

Why newsletters? There are a lot of reasons. Let me list the readers' reasons: 1) time constraints; 2) attention span; 3) ease of reading or skimming; 4) timeliness; 5) specificity; 6) ease of lending; 7) personalism of communication; 8) ease of filing; 9) ease of reviewing; 10) action-orientation.

Now let me list the advantages for the publisher: 1) time constraints; 2) research limitations; 3) timeliness; 4) specificity; 5) training programs; 6) name identification (personal and institutional); 7) variability of the number to be printed; 8) local production; 9) costs of mailing; 10) reinforcement for sermons; 11) reminder of institution's existence; 12) personalism of communication; 13) speed of publication; 14) action-oriented; 15) division of labor factor; 16) national ministry becomes possible.

Almost all of these benefits can be achieved by means of a tape ministry, but tapes have distinct limitations, most notably their cost of production and distribution. The newsletter is much less expensive per person reached.

CHRISTIAN READERS Christian readers don't read very much. Anyone who has read Mortimer Adler's book, *How to Read a Book* (1939) — and anyone who expects to be a writer had better read it — knows how difficult it is to read analytically. Few people ever learn how, including college graduates. He draws on his experiences from the college classroom — the pre-World War II college classroom, when things were far better — to prove his point. Readers are used to simple, passive reading. They read the sports pages of the newspaper, or possibly brief articles in magazines, but seldom do most Americans, including Christians, read a 400-page book, other than novels. The newsletter, even when dealing with difficult material, is less foreboding to the reader, since newsletters are short. A 4-page report, even if a bit technical, is not the threat to the reader that a book is. He may tackle the newsletter; he probably won't tackle a book on the same topic.

The reader believes that he has no time. Women are too busy with children, and men are too busy with business. Everyone is too busy watching television. The writer has to compete with the brain-mushing effects of modern television. The newsletter is a better competitor.

Christians need to be educated, yet you cannot start their educations with 400-page books. You have to begin with their present level of achievement and their present level of motivation. Newsletters are motivational in a way that books are not, since they are issue-oriented and immediate.

You can educate readers step by step. Newsletters can be used in a systematic educational program, such as a doctrinal training program. Or they can be used to alert people to important current events in the church or the world. There are many applications, but the key fact to remember is this: *they are effective because they are read*. It does little good to write if no one reads, except as a self-improvement exercise. The chief goal of writing is to be read.

If many people in the church are reading a newsletter on a regular basis, they will tend to draw others into the circle of readers. Peer pressure is far better as a motivating force than endless reminders from the pulpit that people ought to read more. They also ought to exercise more, spend more time with the kids, fix up the church, and evangelize their neighbors. There are lots of things they ought to be doing. What they will wind up doing is whatever is traditional, easy, and acceptable to their peers. By getting many people reading, the writer encourages others to begin doing something which most people in history haven't had the ability, opportunity, or leisure time to do: read.

PASTORAL GOALS All right, let's not shilly-shally around. Pastors want more money, more influence, more people to take over the cruddy jobs around the church, a larger building, less debt, a steadier source of income for the church, a new evangelism program, more informed members, less bickering among the elders, a good reputation outside the local church, and potential employment opportunities if they can't get their present churches on their feet. Newsletters can provide all of these. I stress the plural. Churches need more than one newsletter.

People outside the church are unlikely to give to a church unless that church is supplying them with something they appreciate. An informative newsletter is something people appreciate. It reminds them, month by month, that the church is alive and well. They become personally linked to the church. Finally, this sense of familiarity can increase the church's income. A newsletter can be a kind of outreach to the uninformed, whose name is legion in American Christianity today.

Pastors, what are your personal interests? Marital counselling? Evangelism? Church fund-raising? Book reviewing? World affairs? Literature? There must be something. If there isn't anything special about your ministry, you should either develop something or get into a line of work to which you can contribute something unique. Find that niche, and then start reading widely in it. Keep your readers informed. Send copies of your letter for six months or a year to those who have expressed some interest in it. Rent mailing lists, if necessary, to identify these people. Take names and addresses when you speak at other churches or at seminars. Take along copies and sign people up. Don't let a speaking opportunity fail to become a source of names and new subscribers.

What kind of newsletter should you consider? There are many possibilities: 1) local church news; 2) world or national events relating to Christianity; 3) specialized letters on common problems, especially family or financial problems; 4) training letters that can be used repeatedly; 5) reprints of classic sermons or other out-of-print materials; 6) letters aimed at informing pastors in a denomination or association; 7) Christian school events; 8) book reviews or other cultural information; 9) motivational letters (evangelism, etc.); 10) devotionals. You can make inserts available to other churches for their bulletins. But *specialization* is important; it is generally a mistake to mix up the categories. You want a *clearly identifiable* newsletter, one which is opened, read, and saved by the readers.

One of the most successful letters is published by the Calvary Temple in East Point, Georgia: *Temple Times*. It reprints sermons, other newsletter articles, and news about the Federal bureaucracy's invasion of Christian liberty. It is sent all over the country. It was the first newsletter to report on the attempt of the IRS to establish racial quotas for Christian schools (August, 1978), and as a result of the newsletter network, over 150,000 letters of protest were generated, and the IRS had to postpone the action (although it is still pending). This indicates how the newsletter industry is becoming a kind of underground information network. The newsletters are the modern equivalent of the Committees of Correspondence during the American Revolution. (Address: Temple Times, 2560 Sylvan Rd., East Point, GA 30344.)

There is no reason why a church can't publish several letters, each aimed at a specific group. There is no reason for the pastor to publish a church news report; that task should be delegated. The pastor should specialize. His teaching ministry should increasingly become a written and tape recorded ministry, with graduates of the training sessions leading the new sessions. A newsletter program allows a continual upgrading of any teaching ministry. The newsletters become inserts for instructional packages later on.

THE CLEARING HOUSE   The church which adopts my issues-oriented program of local evangelism can use newsletters as an integral program of follow-ups. This program is outlined in *The Journal of Christian Reconstruction* (Winter, 1980-81): "Evangelism." Send $7.50 to: Journal of Christian Reconstruction, P.O. Box 158, Vallecito, CA 95251. In this program, local canvassers contact residents, block by block, neighborhood by neighborhood, with a questionnaire geared to specific topics of interest to activist Christians: abortion, national defense, inflation, etc.

They find out what the "hot buttons" are in the community. Then the local church begins to mail a specialized newsletter three times a year or so that deals with *each* of the most popular topics. The church uses its timely newsletters to follow up with those identified as concerned citizens. This is single-issue targeting, but it works. You use the issue which most concerns a citizen to interest him in a total world-and-life view.

Your newsletter program can be geared to attracting outsiders to the church's ministry. It can also be geared to strengthening those within the camp. What we need is for several pastors to specialize in special-interest areas, so that they can exchange letters with others of a similar vision. Each can pull items from other letters, or use the other man's letter in his own publication schedule. If we had 20 writers who could produce a single-interest report three times a year, those pastors co-operating in the exchange could put their own masthead on a report produced by another pastor and mail it out under the local church's banner. No restriction on using the information in any letter would apply to others in the network who were also contributing letters to the group. Special interest letters could be produced by 20 men, and 20 churches would then be in a position to produce reams of material for the various age and interest groups within the community at large, and also within the local congregation.

A monthly magazine that covers the high technology revolution in newsletter publishing, especially the "graphics" aspect of the field—low-cost microcomputers, laser printers, "software" (programs), layout—is

> Personal Publishing
> 549 Hawthorn
> Bartlett, IL 60103 $30/12 issues

The costs of typesetting are beginning to drop as a result of computerization. With a capital investment of as little as $6,000, it is now possible to produce camera-ready copy which looks professionally typeset.

PRODUCTION You need an electric typewriter, preferably an IBM Selectric III or its equivalent. I recommend the "Letter Gothic" typewriter element. Mimeograph your letter, or offset print it (preferred). Typeset it if you can find someone locally who will do it for a reasonable fee (anything under $25 per page in late-1985 was reasonable). Print extra copies for future distribution. The standard format of 8½ by 11 inches is good, although 11 by 17, folded (like I.C.E.'s *Biblical Economics Today*) looks better. It's usually more expensive to print, however.

Even better, get a microcomputer, such as a Leading Edge Model D ($1,495), an IBM PC, or an Apple Mcintosh ("Fat Mac" model). If you do, your writing and record-keeping will be vastly simplified.

If a church finances a church news bulletin and a current affairs report, it's doing well. Better the current affairs report (along the lines of *Temple Times*) than a local church newsletter, if you can afford only one.

We need as many churches in the program of publication as possible. As the tightening grip of the

State sets in, the independent newsletter network will take on ever-growing importance. The existence of Xerox machines and mimeograph machines poses a major threat to any government that would attempt to centralize authority in this country. Communications are far more decentralized in free societies than in tyrannies.

One way of staying out of the limelight of the Federal bureaucracy, if you are a small or new church, is to *avoid applying for IRS-approved church status*. The Post Office requires such approval for its non-profit bulk mail rate. It is wiser to *use the more expensive second class mailing permit which is available to anyone* who mails out 200 at a time. That way, the IRS isn't alerted to the formation of a new church. The IRS does not have to approve your church for it to be tax immune. By applying for exemption, you identify yourself. Better to pay the higher mailing costs and preserve a greater degree of invisibility.

Another advantage of newsletters is that you can stick in a reply envelope for contributions. You can also offer books or other materials in flyers that accompany the newsletter. Warning: if you mail using the non-profit, third class bulk rate, any enclosure must be limited to some organization that also has the legal right to mail on the third class, non-profit basis. Piggybacking is illegal. But an enclosure is legal if you pay the extra money to mail second class for one mailing.

MAILING LISTS A revolution has taken place in fund-raising over the last decade. The advent of the computerized mailing list has made it possible for churches and especially parachurch organizations to target new sources of financial support. The enormous costs of "shotgunning"—radio, television, newspaper display advertising, etc.—have made it prohibitively expensive for smaller ministries. It is costly to announce the existence of a program to tens of thousands of people who really are not that interested, in order to locate and motivate a few hundred who are.

There are ways around the problem. One way is to develop a "phone-in" ministry, where a daily prayer or message is presented. You can advertise the existence of the phone number cheaply enough. Then, at the end of each message, there is a 15-second pitch to mail in for something at a P.O. Box. I built up *Remnant Review* in the early years from 50 subscribers to about 450 by giving a weekly telephone update on gold, silver, and the money supply. I could run a one-column-inch ad in the Los Angeles *Times* for $50, and I always generated four or five $45 subscriptions from each ad. That was cost-effective advertising. But it was a financial newsletter I was selling, not the gospel. Motivating people to respond to an appeal to the gospel takes longer and is not immediately self-financing. However, I still recommend the 24-hour a day recorded message. Code-a-Phone sells some good equipment, or you can rent another unit monthly from the telephone company.

To get the phone-in ministry to work, you need to get the caller to respond in some way. The idea is to target the audience. The newspaper ad is your "shotgun." The caller self-targets himself and calls in. Those who are not interested drop out. Those who are interested will probably call again. *The goal is to use the messages to screen the audience.* Those who finally respond to an offer are far hotter prospects. They represent what the sales industry calls "qualified prospects."

The recorded message is somewhat more personal than the printed page. The human voice has a greater degree of personalism. But people are not going to walk in the church door just because of the tape, unless the tape does something related directly to church services, such as offer a brief summary (with tantilizing questions) about next Sunday's sermon. What people will normally respond to is the offer of literature of some kind. They may hesitate to schedule a visit with the minister, but they are willing to take the next step: writing for a free tract, newsletter, or whatever.

The person who responds to an offer has taken an important first step. He has requested something. You are not shoving anything down his throat. This is very important. Your goal is to bring the person into fellowship on a step-by-step basis. He needs to know at each stage that he is initiating the next step. Your job is to encourage him to take each step. But you need to do this on a cost-effective basis. You should not waste church resources.

With a mailing list, you can target your audience. You can mail questionnaires. You can contact the person to interview him. This enables you to get some idea of his needs and interests, his opinions on matters of life and death, business and leisure. But the more complex the data, the more difficult it is to keep track of him. This is where the microcomputer comes in handy.

Furthermore, you need to send out newsletters, tracts, or other materials to show him the relevance of Christianity. (This will be difficult for churches that do not see the relevance in every area of life of the gospel.) How can you do this effectively?

The first, least expensive step appears to be the old "shoebox" system. You need a card file of 3 by 5 inch cards. These are purchased least expensively at a local college or junior college, rather than in an office supply store. Then you need access to a photocopy machine. You need to run off labels with the person's name and address. One goes on the I.D. card (alphabetical), and perhaps another on a "topical interest" card, if you have identified him to that extent. This way, you can get an idea of what topics most interest readers.

You keep the other sheets of labels in reserve, for mailing purposes. You need to put on your envelopes this message: "Address Correction Requested." The Post Office will send a dead letter back, but at a fee. This keeps your list up to date. Problem: corrections on your master sheets can be a hassle, once the list goes over 300 names or so. You have to paste on new addresses over the slots on the master sheet (33 names per sheet, e.g., Avery label sheets). Then you have to run off a new set of sheets. Or you need a separate sheet of corrected addresses, but then you have trouble with zip codes (which you need in sequence if you mail bulk rate). The zip codes must be sorted, then arranged numerically.

I recommend a mailing at least once a month, to remind readers that you are still around. A church newsletter aimed at topics of general concern is important. You should not be sending out an "in-house" letter to those outside the church family. You must demonstrate your relevance.

You also need a mailing list to announce special meetings, a conference, a movie, or other occasional programs. If you have the person's phone number on your data file, it helps. But you do not want it on the actual mailing label that goes in the mail.

Not many churches will ever develop a mailing list the size of Calvary Temple's in East Point, Georgia. The *Temple Times* goes out to over 10,000 people. But there is always the possibility that your church will develop a list of 2,500, if you work at it all the time. Any time you go over 500, you have to start thinking about computerizing.

CONCLUSION The newsletter is a new tool of communication. Why shouldn't your church get one started?

And if your church isn't interested, why don't you do it personally?

22

THE TAPE MINISTRY

"Some ministers have used tapes effectively. Most of them, from what I have observed, have not."

It takes a great deal of effort to produce a competent sermon. Since pastors invest the time and effort to get educations that enable them to produce decent sermons, plus the time and effort invested in each sermon, it seems foolish to waste the results. It should be clear that while "the walls have ears," church members sometimes don't. Complex sermon outlines are lost on people who are not trained to listen carefully. The kind of memorization described in *Beside the Bonnie Briar Bush*—a novel about the Scottish church of the last century—is no longer common in today's congregations.

Then there are the shut-ins, or the vacationers, or the people who will join the church in ten months or ten years. What about their needs? What about

THE TAPE MINISTRY **205**

those who live in another region? Pastors with a unique outlook on the Bible may have a considerable
audience in distant homes. Some ministries are
noted more for their tapes than for their congregations. Col. Bob Thieme of Houston pioneered the
tape ministry, and Albert Martin of New Jersey has
built up a large following.

It is obvious that the cassette tape has brought a
technological revolution to the churches. Some ministers have used tapes effectively. Most of them, from
what I have observed, have not.

LAZINESS It takes time to develop a successful
church tape ministry. It also takes more care in
preparing sermons. If people are going to listen to
sermons over and over, or if others who are more
careful listeners start subscribing, then flaws in the
presentations will become public knowledge. Some
pastors prefer not to let their actual abilities be
broadcasted widely.

Then there is the problem of getting someone to
produce the tapes. It takes a considerable capital investment. The tape reproduction equipment is expensive, and these units must be maintained. Also, few
pastors know which units are the "state of the art" in
any price range. Not many parishioners are sure,
either. So mistakes are easy, unless someone devotes a
lot of time to reading up on what machines are best
for a particular church ministry and church budget.

MARKETING Tapes just do not sell themselves. I
have a successful tape business, but it is geared to

financial advice. I can charge more because I am providing advice which (presumably) pays the buyer back in dollars. Even so, I am only guessing about the future potential for expanding the business. I also have a very large subscriber base to which I can advertise my tape services very inexpensively. So my case is not normal.

I know of few tape ministries that are larger than 50 tapes per week. Yet it takes hundreds to make it commercially profitable. Tapes must be advertised, either by word of mouth (the least expensive, and the most rare), or by renting mailing lists, or by encouraging church members to buy them. Cults and sects have a better market, since their audiences are geographically dispersed, and its adherents become dependent on information from headquarters. But to the extent that a minister's theology is explicit, he has differentiated himself from most other ministries. He has a better opportunity to market his tapes.

Initially, the market is local. A few congregation members may want the tapes. A set can be produced for shut-ins. A set can be produced for training. If the minister speaks at conferences, he can market tapes there. But normally, the initial audience is limited to those who have heard him speak in person at some point.

TRAINING Churches that rely heavily on formal instruction to screen members have a built-in need for tapes. We live in a society with few careful readers. People like to absorb information more passively than by reading. We meet their needs by means of cassette tapes, possibly coupled with printed training outlines or other teaching materials.

Every pastor who expects to be burdened by marital counselling sessions needs first to produce a series of preliminary tapes geared to general principles of righteous living. Then he needs a second or third series on specific family counselling problems. These should be given to prospective counselees before the actual face-to-face counselling begins. It saves vast quantities of time, since the fundamentals have been reviewed by the counselees in advance. Even if they have forgotten most of the tapes—90% of the information will be gone in 24 hours—the information can be recalled during counselling more rapidly. It is foolish to meet face to face when problems could otherwise have been solved in advance by means of a carefully produced tape series.

Pastors are short of time. People see the pastor as a source of free counselling. At zero price, there is greater demand for his time than supply of his time. The tapes increase the cost to the user by forcing him or her to sit down, take some notes, give some thought to the problems, and then show up for counselling. If users are unwilling to invest the time in listening to tapes, then they are either in the middle of a life-and-death crisis, or not really deserving of any free time at all.

What about tapes on the history of doctrine, or the catechism, or on the confession of faith? What about courses on the doctrine of the church? Why should pastors spend endless repetitive hours teaching the basics of the faith to newcomers, when the newcomers could listen to tapes in a few afternoons, or driving to and from work, or while cleaning the kitchen? Shouldn't the fundamentals be put on tape, in a simple form, with the detailed instruction coming later on, once the listeners have a grasp of the basics?

When pastors treat their own time as a free good, their parishioners will do the same. Pastors of large churches have assistant pastors to take care of the personal problems of most members in most instances. But to make good use of his time, the pastor of a small church has to find substitutes for a team of assistant pastors. His time should not be devoted to any project for which a substitute — a less expensive substitute — is economically possible. Screening should be done more mechanically, by means of tape teaching.

QUALITY PRODUCTION The audio cassette tape, being cheap, is used by many people. Yet few people really ever listen to the tapes produced by cheap hand-held machines, with their pitiful built-in condenser microphones. The reproduction is atrocious. These are the sound equivalent of the 1898 Brownie camera. You simply would not want to spend time listening to them. You could not hear these lectures in a car, given the noise of the engine and traffic. A cheap cassette tape recorder is a toy for actual recording.

Something worth doing at all is worth doing well. Never use a cheap mimeograph machine and a manual typewriter, when you can use an IBM Selectric III and an offset press. Never use an IBM Selectric III when you can use a microcomputer and a good word processing program. Use the best tool you can afford in order to make the products look professional and to save you time. Cheap is seldom best. I am tired of seeing those who do have the truth at their disposal continue to proclaim this truth in forms that are an embarrassment, which look as though total incompetents had produced them. It is not glorifying to God. Christians need more pride in their workmanship. Quality counts.

When it comes to audio tapes, two pieces of equipment are vital. First, a high quality *microphone*. This will do more to improve the quality of the product than any other piece of equipment. Good quality units are sold by Shure, Sony, Sennheiser, Electro-Voice, and other companies. Expect to pay $80 to $250 for a good mike. Second, get a good cassette *tape deck*. Sony, Aiwa, Technics, Akai, Superscope, and many other companies produce suitable units for $250 to $600. Pick up a copy of *High Fidelity* or another magazine aimed at the stereo equipment market. Look at the ads. You will get a feel for what is available. Any unit with Dolby circuitry (especially the new Dolby C), with wow and flutter under .08%, and push-button controls, is fine. Auto-reverse is convenient, but the sound reproduction is not as sharp. If you use auto-reverse, use tapes that don't have plastic lead-in sections at each end.

One other item is useful: a *graphic equalizer*. It can be "tuned" to filter out low rumbles, such as the church's heater or air conditioner. This makes it easier to play in an automobile, too. The mid-range frequencies, where the human voice operates, are "punched out" far more effectively. Expect to pay $100-$200.

A minimum investment to produce decent master tapes is about $400. It would be nice to get started immediately by recording good, clear master tapes, whether or not you plan to market the tapes. *The quality of the master will determine the quality of the reproduction.* The reproduction is never quite as good as the master.

What is absolutely not acceptable is a master produced by a battery-powered cassette recorder with a cheap plastic mike. Forget about these as anything more than play-back units. They are useless for serious recording. The church has to put some capital into proper recording equipment.

High-speed tape duplicators can cost anywhere from $300 up. A master tape is placed in one slot, and anywhere from two to eight "slave" tapes are placed in the "reproduction" slots. It takes only a couple of minutes to produce several tapes. These units require regular maintenance. Wollensak is a popular brand. Buy a high-speed rewinding machine, too, so that the tapes are sent out "ready to play." The duplicator should be used for duplicating, not rewinding tapes. Be sure to set up a comprehensive record-keeping system, including topical information for each tape. Buy a computer and a data base program (ZyIndex is the best).

COSTS A tape ministry does have one great advantage over other media forms: you only produce as many copies as you have orders for. You do not have to risk ordering a hundred in advance, and

THE TAPE MINISTRY **211**

then sit on unsold inventory. You can produce a good quality tape for about $1.25 to $1.50, depending on quantity ordered. Large orders would cost about $1.00, plus postage to get your tapes back to you. This means that you send a company the master, and the firm then turns the master into a specified amount of tapes.

The advantage with having an outside producer make the tapes is that he makes the initial capital investment, keeps the equipment maintained, and guarantees the quality of the tapes. He also buys (or rents) the computer that prints up the tape labels. This keeps the church's initial costs much lower. The disadvantage is the loss of time.

Volunteer labor seldom works well. You are never quite certain of product quality and fast production. If someone in the church does it for pay, make certain that you keep getting outside bids, so that you know that the amateur inside the church is not overcharging you. Blank C-60 tapes in bulk, for example, cost about 50 cents each.

The tapes can be used for several purposes, as I have mentioned. Not every tape may be worth saving, except in the form of a master. Not every series is worth reproducing, but some series should be permanently available for listening. A master tape should never leave the church's premises. It should be kept in a master file, and used only (if then) when people come in to listen to cassettes. The church library room should have a playback machine and a pair of lightweight earphones for private listening.

Use high quality tapes for the master: Scotch;

Maxell UD; TDK AD Series; or other brand equivalents. Stay away from 120-minute tapes (stretching, breaking). Put only one sermon on a tape: easier cataloging, circulation, etc. If you have to fill up a tape, put on some explanatory material after the sermon is over. Or add questions and answers, if it is from a Bible study. (Use a separate high quality mike for the audience's questions.)

The rule is this: put your money into the "front end" of the production process, meaning the mike, tape deck, and cassette masters. This gives you the quality master tapes. You can buy top quality reproducing equipment later on. In the meantime, you can contract out the production job with an independent producer.

23

THE COMPUTER

"It is time to take advantage of the power that inexpensive computer technologies have delivered to middle-class people and their organizations."

You have heard a lot about the computer revolution. Adam Osborne's little paperback, *Running Wild*, describes how it took place, 1975-80. You may be thinking about what it can do for your church. If you have not thought about it, now is the time to begin.

The processing of data is imperative. We need greater speed, reduced cost, and simple-to-use equipment. At last, we are getting it. The best computer deal for the money in late 1985 is the Leading Edge Model D, for about $1,495 (retail). You will also need a printer ($400-$1,500) and operating programs ("software"). Prices keep dropping. If you pay retail, demand full set-up and two hours of instruction, minimum. Wholesale prices are 20% less.

For maximum availability of programs and easily available repairs, the IBM PC or PC AT (but without the built-in hard disk drive—cheaper ones are available) probably would be best. There are many IBM "clones," or look-alikes. Compaq is a good unit. So is Leading Edge. But IBM has set the microcomputer standard.

My favorite word-processing program is Word-Perfect. WordPerfect is available for $250 from 47th Street Computer, 36 E. 19th St., New York, NY 10003, or call 800-221-7774. Huge discounts for popular computer programs!

The advantages a computer offers to a *growing* church program cannot be overestimated. Consider the following fields: mailing list development and maintenance, word processing, publishing, budgeting and records, and a legal defense program (see "Brush Fire Wars.") Churches that ignore the benefits of a computer may wind up paying far more in *forfeited opportunities* than the computer would cost. (What the tool offers deacons is remarkable: the ability to help struggling families think about the family budget, *design a budgeting program*, and a means for housewives to manage it monthly. Could each family help finance the computer by donating money for time used for better budgeting?)

The microcomputers are powerful tools. As software improves—and thousands of geniuses, all looking for a profit, are out there developing new programs—the data-handling of existing "toy" computers will escalate rapidly. They are "toys" only because the programs are poor. Electronically, they represent a revolution, today. Now that IBM, Hewlett-Packard, and other computer giants have entered the field once dominated by Radio Shack and Apple, the market will expand, which means that software will improve dramatically.

WORD PROCESSING The $1,000 typewriter is really obsolete. By late-1984, it was possible to buy a very useful portable—well, at 20 to 25 pounds, moveable—computer for under $1,000. These units include a word processing program, a mailing list program, and other software. Couple one of these with a fast printer like the Epson LX-80 (in the $300 price range) and a letter-quality printer (anywhere from $500 to $2,000), and you have a powerful tool. A good letter-quality printer is the Panasonic KX-P3151 (around $650). Even less expensive systems are now available: under $700 for everything. But you get what you pay for. To spend less than $2,500 in 1985 is probably unwise. You can put sermons, outlines, quotations, Bible references, information from huge, commercially inexpensive data storage banks (UPI, Wall Street Journal, and library information), and anything else on a little plastic disk. You can recall these data by topic, or date, or writer. You can format them into paragraphs, and have the machine shift them around. The better word processors have built-in spelling checkers, and SSI's WordPerfect even has a synonym thesaurus. Writing is a lot easier today. A Hewlett-Packard

LaserJet printer ($3,000) and the PostScript program ($500) allow you to create camera-ready newsletter copy. In short, a revolution in newsletter writing, article writing, and book production is here — for under $3,000.

Say you want to write up weekly sermons. You put them into the computer, just by typing (which allows you to type far faster, by the way). Then you decide to update them, correct them, and put them into a book. You just call back the originals, make the corrections electronically, push a button, and get copy out of your printer. Or you can locate a typesetting company that allows your computer to talk directly over the phone to their typesetting computer. Presto: you can demand about a 30% discount (they pay no one to type the manuscript into the computer), and the total entry time is about an hour, possibly less. Within days, you have in your possession camera-ready copy, without spelling errors (thanks to your electronic dictionary), and formatted by your professional typesetter. A book can go from raw sermons to a finished product in less than two months — possibly a month, if the book printing company co-operates.

CHURCH BUDGETS Want to know where the money is going? Want to be able to budget more effectively? Want to be able to see graphically where the money is going? Want to be able to call up the names of everyone who has donated over $400, or $1,237.58? You can get an instant report from a microcomputer.

Want to send out year-end reports to each member telling him how much he gave, for his tax records (or conscience)? Easy with a computer. Your secretary can do it in an afternoon. Or a deacon can.

CONCLUSION   No church can afford not to have a computer. Buy an IBM PC or "clone." If you can afford $3,000 for a "Bernoulli Box" from Iomega— the best "hard disk" mass-storage system—so much the better. A Hewlett-Packard LaserJet ($3,000) is magnificent. But get started. A revolution has hit the communications field. To ignore it now is to retreat into impotence. Churches need computers: for research (electronic data bases available through the phone lines), for budgeting, for sermon preparation, for scheduling events, for developing mailing lists, and for producing books and newsletters. It is time to take advantage of the power that inexpensive computer technologies have delivered to middle-class people and their organizations.

24

THE CASE FOR A
SATELLITE T.V. RECEPTION DISH

**"What we need is a technological "end run"
around today's entrenched, centralized,
humanist institutions."**

Isolated individuals need to know that they are not alone. The isolation of churches and Christian day schools today is very great. There are a few co-ordinating organizations, but they are very weak. A good way to go bankrupt is to mail unsolicited materials to churches or Christian schools. Headmasters have not been willing to fight until their own schools are being attacked. By then, it is too late. The *Sileven case* in Nebraska is the first one in which this pattern of isolation was broken.

We need to examine the cause of Sileven's notoriety. One word describes the difference: *television*. Several of the "electronic churchmen" devoted time on their shows to Sileven's plight. This media coverage did for Sileven what it did for Martin Luther King. It brought to light what the bureaucrats were doing. I was amused at a 1982 ABC TV report. They interviewed one woman, a supporter of the local public school, who said, "I think Nebraska's affairs should be run by Nebraskans, not all these outsiders." This was the same argument Southern whites used in 1962, the "outside agitators" argument. Television coverage made the difference for King. It could make the difference for Christians who want to recapture the nation.

The existence of satellites and cable channels has at last broken the hold of the major TV networks. The level of information provided by a 30-minute interview is far greater than that provided by a 2-minute news snippet. News snippets are designed to hold an impersonal audience's attention long enough to sell a percentage of them some soap. There is no dedicated group of viewers who are emotionally committed to an anchorman. On the other hand, there are millions of viewers who are personally committed to one or another of the electronic churchmen. Thus, they will sit in front of the screen and listen to a lengthy interview, and even try to understand it. *This puts a major educational tool into the hands of Christian leaders* — a tool which the humanists cannot match on television because of the "least common denominator" principle which governs the Nielsen rating wars.

The lever of television gives the local Christian soldier hope. He knows there is a potential army of supporters behind him, if he gets in a difficult situation. His supporters can be mobilized rapidly and inexpensively if a particular electronic churchman gets his case before the viewers. The problem of anonymity which the local Christian pastor faces in any confrontation with the bureaucrats can now be overcome overnight. This is what Martin Luther King discovered, and it led to the creation of a successful resistance movement in 1956. *Bureaucrats run from adverse publicity the way cockroaches run from light.* This weakness must be exploited by Christian activists.

The very existence of the CBN satellite in itself is a mobilization tool of great importance. It is safe to say that few men are willing today to take the risks necessary to stand up to the various state and Federal bureaucracies. *The very presence of the satellite gives CBN an important edge in getting its people involved in Christian activism.* Without a means of publicizing a crisis, few pastors will take a stand. The CBN-mobilized leaders could easily take positions of leadership locally that other pastors would not dare to take, since they would not have the potential back-up of the CBN Satellite. The satellite is like a howitzer on a battlefield in which Christians have been fighting with pistols and slingshots. And now other Christian ministries are getting their own satellite channels.

Men need motivation. The existence of the satellite network offers men motivation. They can join together in a co-ordinated effort to roll back humanism at every level. This is the approach I call *brush-fire wars.* It can work well for legal resistance, but it can also work for political action, education, and almost everything else. It is a fundamental tool of resistance. But it takes a combination of *centralized strategy* and *local mobilization and execution*.

THE FULCRUM Those who have been most successful in developing the lever of satellite communications and cable TV distribution have been skilled practitioners of media communications. Understandably, there has been a tendency to emphasize the impact of the media. But a medium needs a message; it is not (contrary to McLuhan) itself the message. The message has, until recently, been limited: personal salvation, personal healing, family solidarity, and musical entertainment.

Those who have been in the "fulcrum production business" have been inept at developing levers. They have not written widely read books, nor have they pioneered the use of TV communications or motion pictures. The few exceptions: the Schaeffers, the various Christian counsellors—Dobson, Gothard, and Adams—and the six-day creationist movement (including the old Moody science films). But with respect to positive programs of Christian reconstruction, there has been no successful program so far— graphically or politically.

What is now needed is a bringing together of the lever and the fulcrum. Those who have built up large audiences must begin to join hands with those who have developed specific programs of reconstruction: education, legal defense, political training, etc. The "electronic churchmen" have got to begin to

target specific segments of their audiences who are
ready for specific programs: first by education, second by organizational mobilization. In short, *we
need feet, hands, and eyes*, and each subgroup within
various large television audiences needs specific
guidance and training in order to become proficient.

There is no doubt that CBN would be better able
to begin this program of specialized training than
any of its competitors — as of early 1985. It has the
broadest audience. Scattered within any given
prime-time audience, there are more people who
might be interested in getting involved in a particular action program. CBN is on the air 24 hours a
day. It can therefore devote specific time slots to
identifying and developing segments of the overall
viewing audience, but without alienating the viewers
as a whole. Also, Pat Robertson, not being a pastor,
is less of a threat to the egos and programs of the nation's pastors.

CBN University offers an institutional base for
launching an educational program. Robertson's
Freedom Council offers an institutional base for the
creation of political education and training. If each
of these two organizations can recruit the services of
outside specialists in the particular areas, then the
expertise of the "fulcrum developers" can be put to
use. I have in mind such non-profit organizations as
the Free Congress Foundation, the Rutherford Institute, the American Vision, the Foundation for
American Christian Education, the Foundation for
Christian Self-Government, the Institute for Christian Economics, the various creation research organ-

izations, Chalcedon Foundation, and other educational groups. A body of explicitly Christian literature in several areas has been produced over the last two decades. These educational resources should be integrated into an overall program of education and mobilization.

In the past, there has been a problem of communication between "lever builders" and "fulcrum builders." The "lever builders" have been fearful of becoming too intellectual, too controversial, and too action-oriented to maintain their large, essentially passive Christian audiences. The risk of controversy has been too great. The "fulcrum builders" have resented pressure from the "levers" to "water down" their message in order to meet the needs and intellectual abilities of mass audiences. They have chosen instead to gather still more footnotes, develop still more complex theories, and publish ever fatter books in the quest for the near-perfect intellectual equivalent of Augustine's *City of God* or Calvin's *Institutes*.

In the providence of God, both sides have been correct, up until now. The levers are longer, and the fulcrums are stronger, than they would otherwise have been had the developers in each camp been too concerned with imitating the other. But now the levers are in place, and the fulcrums are as ready as they need to be at this moment in history. Christian viewers are not nearly so passive these days. They see clearly the threat of humanism for the first time. Therefore, it is time to meet the newly felt needs of these viewers. There is always a need for larger au-

diences and more footnotes, but there is a far greater
need today to get the existing footnotes in bite-sized
portions to the existing hungry multitudes. Christ
fed the multitudes with two fish and five loaves of
bread; we can feed them with our existing body of
materials. While they are digesting what we can
deliver today, the fulcrum experts can crank out
more footnotes.

THE "TECHNOLOGICAL END RUN" The humanists
have captured the mainline denominations, the
universities, the major news media, the entertainment media, and the public schools. In short, *humanists have captured the giant institutions*. But look at what
is happening. The generalized institutions are losing
their share of the market. What is clearly taking
place is a shift: *from the generalized to the specialized*,
from the large to the small. *Life* and *Look*, along with
the original weekly *Saturday Evening Post*, did not survive. The proliferation of special-interest magazines
and newsletters has enabled advertisers to target
specific audiences and increase their revenues per
advertising dollar spent. Now the same phenomenon
is taking place in the television industry. Like the
Model T Ford, which could not compete once
General Motors offered five or six cars with numerous models, so is the modern TV network. The networks look strong today, just as the Model T looked
in 1914. Looks are often deceiving.

The humanists captured the national political parties, but today we find that single-interest voting patterns are tearing the national parties apart. Direct-

mail campaigns allow these groups to target their audiences, producing more votes per invested dollar, and more ulcers per elected politician. What Alvin Toffler has predicted in *The Third Wave*, and what John Naisbitt has predicted in *Megatrends: Ten New Directions Transforming Our Lives*, is the coming decentralization. In short, in the face of excessive centralization and statism, we are seeing a countertrend, or better put, multiple countertrends. We are being given an opportunity to attain a better balance between centralism and localism.

Christians are in an excellent position to take advantage of this reversal. Christianity is decentralized — indeed, "fragmented" better describes our condition. If the Christians can assemble themselves into loosely organized but well trained special-interest blocs, while today's centralized humanist culture is disintegrating, the result could be *the creation of a new cultural synthesis*, one based on biblical law rather than some version of humanistic natural law, meaning a version of the myth of neutrality.

What we need, therefore, is *a technological "end run" around today's entrenched, centralized, humanist institutions*. We have begun to do this in television. The development of an alternative information network through newsletters has also made an impact. The development of direct-mail lists has increased our ability to get a specific message to a specific audience. We have a real edge in communications. The Christian day school movement has made a substantial dent in the humanist monopoly of information. Where we have not yet been successful is in the areas of higher education, political training, and legal defense.

As the number of Christian broadcasting alternatives expands, we will be able to create a new educational system. Communications are crucial. When Christian broadcasters know that they can reach an audience of thousands of churches, each armed with a satellite reception dish and several videocassette recorders, they will be able to restructure modern Christian education, including political education. The monopoly of the humanist media will be definitively broken. The sooner your church buys a reception dish, the sooner this monopoly will be destroyed.

Since late 1982, several part-time "networks" have sprung up. Robert Tilton's is the largest, the Word of Faith Church's network. It is received by over 1,800 local churches. This will be imitated. A revolution in Christian mobilization is imminent. Buy a dish.

What size? The larger the diameter, the better the reception. The farther north you live, the larger the dish you need. Never buy a dish smaller than 8 feet in diameter. I prefer a 10-foot dish. In the north, you need a 12-foot dish. Also, I recommend a power rotor. Getting out at 10 P.M. in December to hand-crank a dish to change channels doesn't appeal to me.

25

OPTIMISTIC CORPSES

"There *is* hope for the kingdom of God on earth, precisely because there is *no* hope for God's people to escape the sting of death."

Few concepts are more important to a man or a civilization than the idea of time. Much of what men and whole societies do in life is influenced by men's views of how much time they have in life. For apocalyptic thinkers, the very idea of time is called into question: time will run out. Eternity beckons.

Secularists have no ultimate faith in time. *Time is man's inevitable victor.* Bertrand Russell, the British philosopher and mathematician, has expressed the faith of the evolutionists quite well: "The same laws which produce growth also produce decay. Some day, the sun will grow cold, and life on earth will cease. The whole epoch of animals and plants is only an interlude between ages that were too hot and ages that will be too cold. There is no law of cosmic progress, but only an oscillation upward and downward, with a slow trend downward on balance owing to the diffusion of energy. This, at last, is what science at present regards as most probable, and in our disillusioned generation it is easy to believe. From evolution, so far as our present knowledge shows, no ultimately optimistic philosophy can be validly inferred" (*Religion and Science* [New York: Oxford University Press, (1935) 1972], p. 81). Man and life are defeated by the second law of thermodynamics, the law of entropy. Our generation may survive man-made thermonuclear holocaust, but only to lose to the ultimate thermonuclear holocaust. The sun will go out.

Obviously, few evolutionists sit around consciously creating their life's work in terms of this philosophy. They know in principle that all meaning will be swallowed up in the meaninglessness of entropy's cold death. Man only can get as much meaning out of life as he puts into it. But from what source does man derive meaning? Only from himself? Then one man's opinion is as good as any other man's opinion. How, then, do we choose between a Hitler and a Gandhi? Relativism can turn into nihilism very fast. So while the specifics of this entropy-based cosmology are not that important, the *general attitude of meaninglessness* filters down into the outlook of evolutionists.

The evolutionist knows that he must die. All men must die. The whole race, and all traces of it, must die. They can build for the long term, however, and modern, Western, scientific evolutionists do build for the future. Humanist civilization is a testimony to their willingness and ability to build for the future. They have borrowed an ethic more properly described as Christian, a future-oriented philosophy, and they have not faced the reality of cosmic meaninglessness too consistently. As they grow more consistent, their implicit relativism will destroy them. But at least the evolutionist knows he must die. He can defer the implications of meaninglessness until a million or a billion years into the future.

How, then, does he try to escape from death? Many ways. One way is to adopt the attitude which says, "I've got five good years left."

FIVE GOOD YEARS This is a very common attitude. Men in positions of authority in one-man outfits, especially non-profit outfits, hold this position quite frequently. As they grow older, they refuse to consider the future of their little organizations. They say to themselves, "I've got five good years left, maybe even ten. No need to start thinking about a successor. No need to worry about a plan for the future. I'll think about all that when I'm at the end of my work. But right now, I've got five good years left."

They have another tendency. They equate their little organizations with themselves. They *are* the organization. Then they equate the organization with civilization's best and most enduring features. But when they die, the organization dies, so civilization will probably die, too. Therefore, in terms of their time perspective, they think they are as immortal as civilization. They take no thought of twenty years from now, for they are convinced that civilization, like themselves, has only about five good years left. After them, the deluge.

Methuselah lived longer than any other man. He died in the year of Noah's flood. (He was 187 years old when he begat Lamech, and 182 years later, Lamech begat Noah [Gen. 5:26-27]. Then, 600 years later, the flood came [Gen. 7:11]. If you add 187, 182, and 600, you get 969 years, which was what Methuselah lived [Gen. 5:27]. He therefore died in the year of the flood.) More than any other man in history, he had the most opportunities to say, accurately, that he had at least five years remaining. Also more than any other man in history, he had the right to say, "After me, the deluge." Yet life went on. A new civilization lay ahead, through the waters of the flood.

Those who assume, as Queen Elizabeth I assumed, that they have five years left, are very short-sighted. Elizabeth refused to name a successor, so her survivors named James I, who turned out to be a disaster for England, as Otto Scott's biography of him demonstrates. Things do go on. They go on with or without any individual. They go on with or without that individual's legacy. The man who continually assumes that five years are ahead of him, so he can safely defer a decision on who or what will survive him, is a short-sighted man. Others will use his legacy to their own advantage, but the less he leaves with instructions for the perpetuation of his capital or work, the more will remain for his heirs—spiritual, genetic, ideological, or bureaucratic—to dispose of as they please. The inheritance survives; the question is: What will be done with it? Survivors decide. Try to train and name your survivors.

CHRISTIAN IMMORTALITY: TRUE AND FALSE

There are literally millions of Christians who equate biblical immortality with physical survival. This may sound ridiculous. Don't all Christians long for eternal life, the life beyond the grave? Yes. However, the vast majority of those who call themselves fundamentalists think they can and will avoid the grave. They expect to be raptured into the heavens, without first tasting the sting of death. They think that they are the members of "the terminal generation," as Hal Lindsey, America's most terminal thinker, has put it. They will be the "lucky" people who will pass from corruption to incorruption without dying (I Cor. 15:51-52; I Thes. 4:15-17). "Go directly to heaven; do not pass 'DEATH.' "

What will they leave behind? Pretribulationist premillennialists think that they will leave behind a world of war, famine, and terror. Then, seven years later, they will be returned to Planet Earth as semi-gods, in fully incorruptible bodies, incapable of death or sin, to rule over those people who still live in corruptible flesh. Post-tribulation premillennialists think they will go through the period of terror, but will be raptured out at the end, only to be returned as semi-gods immediately after their transformation into incorruptible, sinless rulers. Amillennialists think that the resurrection takes place at the same time as the rapture, and that the final judgment follows. There will be no era of semi-god status, mixed in with people who had not been raptured as saints. The rapture means the end of time in the amillennialist perspective. No earthly, sin-influenced millennium follows the rapture.

In any case, whatever is left behind is not worth much, compared with whatever follows. It is not worth saving. It is not a down payment on the future era of bliss. It is only the stained rags of life which we are all trying to escape. What we leave behind, in short, is bio-degradable trash. Our legacy will rot.

Christians seek immortality. They want to avoid death. They are generally convinced that the end is in sight, that there is "light at the end of the tunnel." The rapture draws nigh. Escape draws nigh. Immortality draws nigh — an immortality which is not stung first by death. Literally millions of Christians believe that they, as members of the terminal generation, will experience this death-free way to immortality. I call this *pessimillennialism*.

OPTIMISTIC FUTURE CORPSES Only one tiny group of Christians firmly believes that they will die. In fact, they rejoice in the fact that there are more years ahead for society than there are for themselves. They know they must plan and build in terms of their own death. They know that someone will read their last wills and testaments, including institutional last wills and testaments. They know that there is no escape, that insofar as life is concerned in our day, nobody gets out of it alive. These people are called postmillennialists. They are *optimillennialists*.

David Chilton, who wrote *Paradise Restored: A Biblical Theology of Dominion* (Reconstruction Press, 1985; $14.95), once remarked that the day he accepted postmillennialism, he finally realized that he was going to die. He said that this awareness was unique. Nobody had ever told him this before. He and his premillennial peers had always believed that they were going to be raptured. He said that this new perspective on his own personal future changed the way he thought about his life's work. Indeed, it had to. One's time perspective is crucial to one's view of work and work's legacy. The problem today with postmillennialism, perhaps more than anything else, is that it is a philosophy of personal, physical death. That sort of philosophy really has a limited Christian market in our era. Marxists have a secularized version of this faith, which is why they are such potent ideological opponents. Most Christians have no such outlook. They prefer not to think about death. They prefer to think about the rapture.

Death is the backdrop of all endeavors by postmillennialists. The death of the sin-cursed body is the starting point. Then the question has to be asked: How should we then live? What kinds of institutions should we build? What kind of education should we impart to our children? How much capital should we invest in long-term projects? What kinds of books should we read or write? How, in short, should we *fight*? What can anyone leave behind that his own death will not swallow up?

Because postmillennialists know that they cannot assume continually that they have five good years left, and that they should assume that their organizations are *not* going to be left behind in a world without the presence of other Christian workers, they have to think about the future. Because they know they will die, they can be optimistic about the future. They know that other Christians will persevere. They know that Christian institutions will survive to serve as salt for a world civilization. Because they will die, they think to themselves, they can build for the earthly future of others who will also die. Because their view of their own efforts is necessarily short run — one lifetime, at most — their view of the *long-term effects of their efforts* is implicitly long run.

No one in this world gets out alive. None of us will be raptured. No institution is left behind without any possibility of extension into the future. God will not pull the plug on history until the whole world is brought under His institutional sovereignty. There *is* hope for the kingdom of God on earth, precisely because there is *no* hope for God's people to escape the sting of death. Postmillennialists can rejoice in their own physical mortality. Their efforts can multiply over time, long after they are dead and gone. They are optimistic. They know, in principle, that they are future corpses. There is no escape. Once this is firmly in one's mind, one can get to work — work for the long haul. By God's grace, the results of such work will survive and prosper.

TO PLANT A TREE When men look to the future, they can make minimal investments that can, if given enough time, become major sources of spiritual or financial capital. If the compounding process begins, and continues over a long enough period, the whole world can be influenced. The fact that we have short lifetimes does not mean that we cannot make long-run investments. In fact, this understanding encourages us to make these sacrifices today. We plant cultural seeds for the church's future.

We derive our meaning from God. Our work on earth survives, if it is good work. It survives in heaven (I Cor. 3:11-15), and it also survives on earth. The Christian who is an optimistic future corpse does not worry that his work will go the way of the evolutionist's work, to be overcome by impersonal entropy. He does not worry about leaving behind a life's work that will be swallowed up in the horrors of the seven-year Tribulation. He looks to God in faith, knowing that Christ will deliver up a completed kingdom to the Father (I Cor. 15:28).

We can plant a tree, and if it is cared for by those who follow us, it will bear fruit. We can plant today, knowing that there is sufficient time, this side of the final judgment, for it to mature. It could be cut down in a war, as any good work can be at any time, but we know it will not for certain be cut down in absolute destruction during a Great Tribulation. That Tribulation took place when Jerusalem fell to the Roman legions in 70 A.D. (Luke 21:20-24). The work of any godly man has a possibility of survival into the distant future. The rate of growth need not be large under such circumstances. Little by little, line upon line, his capital investment can prosper year by year. His spiritual successors can see to its care and maintenance.

Those who view God's history as a giant scythe which will cut down all the works of Christians on the final day (or rapture) except for internal, "spiritual" works, cannot plant cultural seeds with the same confidence, and therefore the same enthusiasm, as those who view themselves as future corpses whose work is long-term capital that can survive. On the day of judgment, the garden produced at last by Christian discipline and Christian capital will not experience a silent spring. It will be a thing of beauty, delivered to the Father by the Son as His fulfilment of the dominion covenant (Gen. 1:28). His people will share in His pride of workmanship. As His stewards, they will have a part in its historical fruitfulness. That fruitfulness will extend into the New Heavens and the New Earth.

[The best introduction to an optimistic view of the future is David Chilton's book, *Paradise Restored: A Biblical Theology of Dominion*, published by Reconstruction Press, P.O. Box 7999, Tyler, TX 75711; $14.95.]

26

HOW MUCH TIME?

"Aim high, aim carefully, and shoot long."

It should be obvious that a suitable strategy for a marathon runner is considerably different from a sprinter's strategy. If you have 26 miles to cover, your pace will be a lot steadier, and you will be called upon to maintain considerably greater reserves of energy. The sprinter will give a lot more attention to the crouch, the starting blocks, and the signal to start. The distance runners do not even bother to crouch; there are no starting blocks; and you never see a false start by those anticipating the starting run. It is endurance, not speed out of the blocks, that will determine the success of the marathon runner.

The Hebrews were promised a kingdom land in Canaan. Yet the promise took several centuries to come true, from Abraham's day to Joshua's, and the period of training involved years of captivity and four decades in the wilderness. So while their advent into the promised land was a sharp discontinuity from the point of view of the Canaanites of Joshua's day, from the point of view of the Hebrews, it was a long-term process. The foundations had been laid between Abraham's era and Joshua's; the seemingly rapid completion of the conquest was possible only because of the centuries of theological, ecclesiastical, and institutional investment that had preceded it.

The kind of institution a person or a group builds depends upon their estimation of the capital, skills, and time available to them. If they are convinced that there is insufficient time to bring the project to its completion, then they have the architect redesign the plans. Similarly, if they are convinced that the skills or the capital available are minimal, they will design the plans accordingly. It is senseless to start construction without estimating in advance the likelihood of its being possible to bring the project to completion (Luke 14:28-30). Furthermore, if a person thinks the structure will be in service for 50 years, he will use one set of construction materials. If he expects it to be in service for several centuries, he will select a different quality of building materials.

Does it make sense to criticize the short-run builder? It depends. The British in the early nineteenth century built their rails with the best, most expensive steel available. It consumed large quantities of financial capital. Americans built their railroads using cheaper materials that were only expected to last a couple of decades. Meanwhile, tremendous gains were made in metallurgy, and by the time the American rails were worn out, they could be replaced with far better rails than the British possessed, and at a far lower expenditure of capital. Throughout the intervening years, the builders had the extra capital to use for other purposes. They "built cheap," and let technology come up with the better product later on. The same thing has happened in our era with computer technology. It is not sensible to "buy ahead" when you buy a computer; increased needs in the future should be purchased in the future, when prices will be far lower and performance will be greater.

But what about the long-run builder? Is he foolish? It depends on whether or not we really have a lot of time remaining to us — collectively, as a race; nationally; or geographically, where we are building our structures. Maybe there were Canaanites who went to considerable expense just prior to the exodus to build family estates that would last 500 years. Not too smart, in retrospect; they were just increasing the capital value of the Hebrews' property. If we expend huge quantities of long-term capital, and discover that it is blown away by short-term forces of history, then we have wasted our capital. However, if we blow away our capital on short-run projects, only to discover that we have run out of money a long time before the end appears, then we have also wasted our resources. It is imperative, then, that we make accurate assessments concerning the time remaining to us.

It should be obvious that in the twentieth century, very few Christian groups think that we have a lot of time remaining. This has drastically influenced the kinds of institutions they have constructed, and are in the process of constructing. (Why these groups continue to encourage pension fund programs and annuities for their pastors is a mystery, but they do. Maybe—just maybe—the administrators of the funds think they can get access to the ministers' money today, and avoid having to pay off later, in the post-rapture period. Of course, the fund managers may decide to invest the funds in terms of this operating assumption, praying fervently that Christ returns in glory before the dollar goes belly-up and the funds go bankrupt. It is my contention that a majority of pension investors and annuity holders living today will learn to their dismay that time has run out for the dollar, not the dispensation.)

In medieval times, communities built cathedrals that were expected to last for a thousand years, and some of them have. Generations of local contributors and craftsmen would add their money, goods, or services to the long-run construction project. These majestic buildings are no doubt being used today by people who do not hold dear the religious beliefs held by the builders, which is the best argument against what they did, but at the same time, these structures attest to the long-run vision they shared, their hope for the future, and their willingness to sacrifice present income for the sake of the beauty which many generations after them would enjoy. If they built their cathedrals for narrowly ecclesiastical reasons— a vision of the church and church worship—then they may have erred, for the church in our day has abandoned the kind of supernaturalism that the builders revered. However, if they built in terms of a broader-based kingdom ideal — an ideal encompassing beauty, majesty, craftsmanship, and architectural skill — then their efforts were not wasted. Of course, it seems likely that they built for both reasons, for the kingdom clearly encompasses the church as an institution, so part of their desires have been frustrated. But time frustrates almost every human vision to some extent, and theirs at least has persevered in the realm of aesthetics. Like the builders of the tabernacle, or Solomon's temple, their efforts were later misused by evil men, but they left a heritage nonetheless.

TRACTS AND TREATISES Is it preferable to spend $10,000 on printing up a million tracts, or is it better to print up 7,500 books? Again, it depends. The tracts will not survive the test of time. The gospel is furthered in a particular era, assuming the tract is actually distributed and read. But the tract is short-lived. Its effects will be brief, except insofar as those converted by its message go on to write more tracts, or evangelize on a face-to-face basis. The printer of tracts knows that the results will be visible soon, or not at all, for a tract is like a shooting star: bright, possibly exciting, but soon dimmed.

The book producer knows that his book may stand the test of time. It may survive and become the foundation of a new movement, a new school of interpretation, the basis of a new civilization. Certainly, Augustine's writings became just that (William Carrol Bark, *Origins of the Medieval World*). So did

Aquinas' books, and Calvin's. Would they have better spent their time writing tracts alone? Would our heritage have been greater? Few people would say so today, I suspect. One thinks of Gregor Mendel, the obscure monastic, working with his peas. No one read his report on genetic variation when it was first published over a century ago in an obscure scientific journal, but his research became the basis of modern genetics a generation later. Was he wasting his time? From what he could see when he died a century ago, he might have been, but he would have been wrong.

Anyone who has looked at the library of a deceased typical pastor discovers very fast that the bulk of his library is worthless. The books on pastoral counseling, on preaching, on psychology, on church management, even on historical topics, are all too often third-rate studies by fourth-rate writers. Their books did no better than a tract, possibly not as well. If the pastor happened to be a theological liberal, and if he collected his books from 1900 to 1930, there may not be a single volume that anyone, liberal or conservative, would read today, except as an historical curiosity. Twentieth-century fundamentalism has done far better with its tracts than its books; its tracts gather converts, but its books gather dust.

One reason for this is the time perspective of modern Christianity. If the end is near, the evangelist seeks the "biggest bang for the short-term buck." He seeks visible converts, filled pews, and an army of tract-passers. While everyone acknowledges that "Explo-72" (or some other crash-program in mass evangelism) is little more than a faded memory in the minds of most American Christians a decade later, and was never even noticed by the vast majority of American pagans in 1972, there is always hope that next year's campaign will gain that last convert, after which Christ will return, either in judgment or secretly, before the Tribulation. The kingdom is not seen as a growing, transforming civilization, into which many are pressing to enter, but as a kind of theological spaceship, into which the remnant is pressing in order to escape some terrible cataclysm. When the last passenger is on board, it will be time for the big blast-off, leaving the world behind. The kingdom as spaceship, like the kingdom as island, or the kingdom as fortress, is a negative conception of the kingdom—a place of refuge, not a civilization for conquest.

CONCLUSION We do not know for certain when the end will come. We must be like long-distance runners who conserve their strength because they are never quite certain until the very end where the finish line is. Yet we must acknowledge that we may not slack off, for our energy is to be conserved for that final "kick" that carries us across the finish line in the lead. We dare not get too far behind. We must not plan for a victory sometime in the distant future, and then neglect the hard realities of keeping up the pace in the present. We need tracts to go with our treatises, and converts for continuity.

The sprinters of the theological world have left very little as an inheritance. Those who have planned to "evangelize Africa in a generation," or "win the youth of the nation by 1976," or whatever, have pursued a demonic goal—demonic because it sidetracks the construction of long-term Christian projects in favor of short-term, unrealizable, and very expensive campaigns that are, of necessity, concerned only with the surface of Christian faith and Christian culture. Better to plan for a long-term program to subdue the whole earth, generation by generation, than to squander our capital in a short-term sprint to save a remnant and then leave the world to the devil. Aim high, aim carefully, and shoot long. Time is on our side because God controls time and has given to His people all the time they need to carry out the terms of the dominion covenant. It will take time for our capital to become totally productive, like the orchard. Maybe that is one reason why God forbids us to eat the produce of the orchard until its fifth year (Lev. 19:23-25): a reminder that we have plenty of time left to enjoy the fruit of our labor. Therefore, get to work planting, today.

27

THE LONG, LONG HAUL

"Two steps forward and one step back is a perfectly reasonable strategy, if you think you have time on your side."

One of the strange anomalies of modern social and political life is the sharp contrast between what conservatives believe and what they actually do, and an analogous contrast between what revolutionaries say they believe and what they actually do. Both sides are inconsistent, and these inconsistencies go a long way to explain why the radicals have been so successful, and the conservatives have not.

Consider the radicals' view of reality. Following Marx, they believe that the institutions of modern life are corrupt. The corrupt environment of mankind is what lies at the root of injustice in social affairs. By reconstructing man's environment, they believe, they can produce a fundamental alteration in the nature of man. All radicals share some version of *environmental determinism*.

Marx, however, went farther than this. He argued that social and political institutions are so corrupt that a revolution is needed to remove the influence of the ruling class. "Revolutions are the locomotives of history," he wrote. The history of man has been the history of class struggles, he declared in the early section of the *Communist Manifesto*. Revolution cannot be avoided. (He made two totally inconsistent and pragmatic exceptions: England and Russia.) Marx held to a religion of revolution. Historical change that is significant must be *discontinuous*. Significant social, economic, religious, and political change must be rapid, all-encompassing, and class-directed. Slow, organic change is not significant; only discontinuous breaks in the continuity of history are socially important in the processes of history.

This same philosophy was basic to the radicals of the French Revolution. It was against such a view of life that Edmund Burke wrote his classic book, *Reflections on the Revolution in France*, which he wrote in 1790, the year following the opening shots of the French Revolution. His argument ran as follows. All meaningful social change is cumulative, the product of organic development. Society is an organic whole, with slow, steady development of its constituent parts. No revolutionary regime can maintain personal, local, and traditional relationships within a society. Any attempt to upset these relationships by force will lead to a rupture of society. Only terror, oppression, and the centralization of the State can impose a revolutionary break on society, apart from war. He predicted the terror of the French Revolution several years before it was visible to the West.

Burke's essay became the touchstone of nineteenth-century conservative social philosophy. A commitment to tradition, organic change, and steady progress was the conservatives' alternative to bloody revolution. Only organic change, Burke maintained, protects human freedom from the grasping reach of the revolutionary State. Only the intermediary institutions—family, church, guild, etc.—can protect a man from the growing power of the State. When all men are defined strictly as citizens—when all men are told that the only membership worth having is their membership in the State—the State will become tyrannical. There is no salvation, personal or collective, by politics. This was Burke's conservative philosophy.

RIVAL PROGRAMS   If you were to read Marx and Burke, you might imagine that Marx's intellectual heirs would have given up the fight long ago. Where is the promised proletarian revolution? Marx wrote to Engels in 1858 that he feared that the revolution might come before he had time to finish his book, *Contribution to the Critique of Political Economy*, which was published in 1859. Not only did the proletarian revolution not come in 1858, we are still waiting for its arrival.

Do the Communists still propagandize? More than ever. Do they still map out long-range strategies for victory? They do. Are the Soviets

devoting huge budgets to military spending, in order
to outpace the West's military machine? They are.
Why do they do it? Shouldn't revolutionaries abhor
the long-term, steady, seemingly relentless task of
building a revolution? Shouldn't they forget the
whole thing and go home? Isn't it futile to devote a
lifetime, or several generations, to the task of producing one overnight transformation of society
through revolution? In short, why is it that the Communists are so dedicated to the discipline of continuity, when their faith rests on an ultimate discontinuity?

On the other hand, what about the conservatives,
which includes most of the evangelical churches?
What is their program geared to? Generally, the conservatives hope and pray for a miracle, usually a
political miracle, and since miracles are in short supply these days, a national political miracle. This
means electing a President of the United States. It is
somewhat different in parliamentary systems, since
the Prime Minister holds his office because his party
has a majority in the parliament. He is there because
numerous local elections have put representatives of
his party into office. But in the United States, the
President may be (and often has been) a lone figure.
The House and Senate can be controlled by a rival
political party. So the main office can be captured by
one campaign—a campaign whose resources have
been devoted to electing one man to office, and not
necessarily his party. (The Presidential campaign of
1972 was the archetype of such an election, when
Nixon siphoned off millions of dollars of Republican

Party funds to assure his re-election, thereby depleting the funds remaining for House and Senate campaigns.)

So the conservatives, who believe in continuity, pray for discontinuous events: Presidential or parliamentary victories every few years. In between, they return to their normal pursuits: family life, business, education, etc. The humanistic liberals believe in salvation by politics, and they devote large quantities of their time, money, and energy to this end. The conservatives specifically do not affirm a faith in salvation by politics, so they tend to be less devoted to the cause of politics. This has produced the anomaly: liberals working for years to achieve a smashing political victory across the boards, and conservatives working sporadically, hoping for an occasional figurehead victory. The liberals staff the bureaucracies and the appointed positions, even when a conservative wins the top office. The liberals have the experience and the dedication to politics; they have the expertise to gain the offices' staff positions. Conservatives lack the trained, dedicated troops to carry through on an occasional political victory, from grass roots to staff positions at the top.

When conservatives gain a victory, they go home. They think they have done their duty for the year, or even for the next four years. They turn away from politics, not having a great deal of faith in politics. The liberals never stop pushing, subverting, or infiltrating. They never go home. Conservatives, because they often have the support of the mass of actual voters on many issues, are capable of electing men through the use of sophisticated direct-mail techniques, but their victory ends the night the polls are closed and the ballots are counted. They can elect men, but they have not demonstrated any ability to lead. They have not followed through. Their ability is limited to the day of the election, not the crucially important ability of staffing the positions and carrying through a legislative program.

In other words, if victory does not come in politics as a result of one act of will, the conservatives aren't that interested in getting involved. Their faith is not in politics, so the extent of their vision is limited by a single electoral victory. They preach continuity, but they act in terms of discontinuity. The liberals and radicals preach discontinuity, and act in terms of continuity. The liberals have won.

THE LOGIC OF CONTINUITY "For which of you, intending to build a tower, sitteth not down first, and counteth the cost, whether he have sufficient to finish it?" (Luke 14:28). We have to face the reality of the costs. We believe in the continuity of work, yet we also believe that God intervenes in the lives and affairs of men. We believe in biblical law, but we also believe in miracles. However, *we* are responsible for implementing the law; God is responsible for the miracles.

The proper strategy for Christian reconstruction is long-term discipline in every area of responsible action. We dig in early and steadily expand our area of influence. Where a person's *heart* is, there he will adopt a philosophy of *continuity*. The farmer working his soil, the businessman developing a market, an inventor developing a working model: here are examples of continuity. Since Christians are called into God's service, they must adopt a program of continuity in their primary area of service.

The shortening of men's time horizons as a result of both premillennialism and amillennialism has contributed to *a decline in competence* among Christian workers and *an increase in reliance upon the miraculous*. If men do not believe that they have a lifetime to develop their skills and capital, let alone to pass down both skills and capital to later generations, they must become dependent upon God's miracles to advance their causes. *As men's time horizons shrink, their quest for "the big pay-off" increases*, since only through such a discontinuity can they expect to advance themselves significantly in a brief period of time. The man who has time can experience steady but slow increases in his capital — however he measures his assets. The man who does not have time cannot afford the luxury of continuity.

COVENANTS AND TIME To count the costs, you must be able to estimate time. Time is a significant factor in assessing true cost. Try to get a home built in half the time; it costs more money. The same is true of almost any investment. The shorter the payout period, the higher the risk involved. Short delivery time schedules cost more.

When men covenant with an eternal God, they must have some idea of what He expects them to accomplish in time and on earth. They must estimate the kind of time horizon God has in mind for His covenanted community, including the sons and daughters of today's faithful remnant. *The covenant stretches across generations*. This is what gives significance to *little triumphs*; they can accumulate over time to produce *extensive results*. The compounding effect requires time, but if you have enough time — and if your time horizon encompasses all the time you have — then you do not need large percentage increases each year in order to achieve your goals. A little each year goes a long way, if you have enough time.

The radicals have grasped this. Marx was convinced that there was a march of progress over time, that the proletarians would inevitably win, and therefore it is worth sacrificing a lifetime to produce the pamphlets and books that would strengthen the proletariat over its long-term struggles. Marx had a vision of history which stretched back to the hypothetical ancient communist agricultural communities. Time was important to him — he thought the timetable for revolution was much shorter than it was — but time was not a threat to him. He could settle for minor victories. So could Lenin. *Two steps forward and one step back* is a perfectly reasonable strategy, if you think you have time on your side.

The conservatives have adopted a philosophy of continuity in some areas of their lives — family, business, church growth, etc. — but not in political affairs. As they lose faith in time, their commitment to continuity will be reduced in whatever areas of ultimate concern that they have. Until they become convinced that time is on the side of righteousness, they will remain ineffective politicians, and they will become less effective in those areas of life that they are willing to sacrifice for over the long haul. Divorce and business bankruptcies will increase as men's time horizons decrease. Men will not "stick it out" for the long haul.

CONCLUSION   Victory is not to the swift, but to those who recognize that they are in a very long-distance marathon race. Who will "go the distance"? Those who see that time is on their side, because they are covenantally subordinate to the God who controls time. They can have a valid faith in programs of continuity, leaving the miracles to God. Because they have time, and a strategy geared to time, they become less dependent on miracles and more dependent on biblical law. This is what Christian maturity is all about. It is what Christian reconstruction is all about. It is what victory is all about.

28

SMALL BEGINNINGS

"Frustration is basic to reconstruction."

For who hath despised the day of small things?
(Zech. 4:10a)

One of the difficult things to imagine is a modern proponent of political liberalism standing up to pass the hat for some local social action project. What he will attempt to do is to create a grass-roots pressure group to promote the financing of the particular project with local taxpayer funds, or better yet, through Federal grants. The political liberal's idea of social action is action to increase the power of the State over local affairs.

The political liberal wants to achieve his goals through political action. His religion is the religion of politics. He is skilled at gaining favors by the State for pet projects. His answers for almost every problem are political: pass a law, enforce a law, get a grant. He enjoys politics. He sees politics as the central activity of a civilization. The State is the central institution.

The political conservative tends to regard politics as simply one activity among many, and the State as one institution among many. His interest in politics is diluted, unless he is a professional whose calling is politics. The strength of the conservative movement lies outside of politics, unlike the strength of political liberalism.

When something needs to be done, the conservative tends to ask himself, "How can it be done at a profit?" A second question is: "How can it be done on a tax-deductible basis?" The third question used to be: "Can it be done locally?" The fact that the third question is not usually asked by conservatives today indicates the extent to which conservatism has been influenced by the reigning political errors of the day.

This leads me to the topic of this chapter, namely, the advantages and weaknesses of the non-statist approach to social problems. If we reject the premise of the statist, then we should have confidence in non-statists approaches to problems. But to overcome the statist ideology of our age, we have to be confident in our ability to succeed without appealing to the State.

RUNNING LEAN Herbert Titus teaches law at CBN University in Virginia Beach, Virginia. This is Pat Robertson's school: Christian, conservative, and privately supported. In the Vietnam war period, Titus was a radical professor at the University of

Oregon. He used to help students obtain draft deferments, as well as oppose the war in other ways. He noticed only years later that almost nobody ever offered to pay him for his assistance. It was assumed by radical students that such assistance was a free good, that it was somehow owed to the beneficiary. This is the typical mind-set of the political liberal.

The same phenomenon affects the bulk of the socialist-interventionist movements of our time. With the notable exception of the Communists, the Left has been generally unwilling to self-finance their programs in this century. They much prefer to get the State to finance them. This has been done, too; the conservative rallying cry, "De-fund the Left," is valid. Ideologically radical organizations have for years been granted millions of dollars, from Planned Parenthood to the Legal Services Corporation.

But at some point, this dependence on the State backfires. Sources of private funding dry up, since everyone knows that the State is writing the checks. For instance, the Left has not developed successful direct-mail campaigns or mailing lists, unlike the conservatives. When public opinion finally turns against the religion of secular humanism, and voters start cutting off the funds, these organizations will lose access to perpetual funding. When the fiat monetary unit finally goes the way of all flesh, what will they use to pay their employees? The government supplies the money, but the money it supplies is Federal money. What happens if Federal money becomes worthless?

Non-statist movements start small and poor. They are decentralized. They must compete for the financial support of a limited number of donors. Most donors are on several mailing lists, and many ideologically conservative groups appeal to them for funding. They have to pick and choose among a large number of ideologically compatible organizations.

This competition tends to keep the conservative and religious groups lean. They cannot afford much waste. If they get fat, a downturn in the economy can cause a crisis. Thus, these groups learn to survive in a competitive market. This trains them in the realities of communication; if they have no message, no packaging, no mailing list, and no distinctive program, they are unlikely to survive, let alone prosper. This keeps them sharp. It keeps them relevant.

There is a price to pay for these benefits: *uncertainty.* Nothing is guaranteed. There is always the threat of disaster looming ahead. The fund appeals may take on a tone of desperation, of continual crisis. People who give money in response to such appeals, and only such appeals, are not the kind of people who make effective long-term associates or backers. The organization which attracts and keeps such donors is hard-pressed ever to admit success. If it does, it risks lower income.

Small religious and conservative organizations are for years confined to a state of total dependence on voluntary contributions. They struggle just to stay alive. They come and go. They frequently do not survive the death of the founders. But they leave behind *a legacy of dissent*, and this legacy eventually makes itself felt when the bankruptcy of the existing establishment becomes obvious, when the State can no longer supply the vote-getting special privileges and funds.

The despair which sets in after years of frustrating losses is natural. It must be resisted. *Frustration is basic to reconstruction.* The seeming imperviousness of the existing social and political order is overwhelming at times. But Gandhi's experience in India should remind us that a lifetime of seeming futility was rewarded with success, at least in the sense that Gandhi achieved his stated political goal, namely, independence from Britain. He ran very lean. Actually, he walked very lean. His march to the sea, his two fasts almost unto death, and his other public relations coups made him a formidable opponent of the entrenched ruling class.

VOLUNTARISM The strength of the non-statist groups, above all, is the commitment of their supporters to the cause. These people are willing to take their hard-earned money, and send it to a ministry they approve of. This is not characteristic of their opposition. They have *real reserves* — reserves of dedication, commitment, and the habit of regular financial sacrifice. The supporters are willing to take a stand. More than this: they are willing to finance a stand.

These groups stay small. They get their message out "by hook or crook," but seldom with support from the established intellectual and religious opinion-makers. But the real opinion-makers are not those who are most visible at the end of a civilization. They are the people who are hidden in the historical shadows, working patiently until the day comes when a cultural crisis creates demand for new opinions.

Look at any urban public (government) school. It is bigger than any Christian school you have ever seen. A typical public high school has more students than any Christian high school in the country. But these schools, for all their bricks and mortar and football teams, are dying. Those inside are getting substandard educations. Yet it is tax-supported education, above all, which is the center of hopes, dreams, and schemes of the priests of humanism. *The public school is humanism's established church, and its influence is fading fast.* State boards of education are literally panicking at the threat offered to them by home schools and small Christian schools. They have good reason to panic. In a century, tax-supported education may well be a relic of the past, swept away by the forces of voluntarism. What will the broken bricks and loosened mortar be worth then?

Defenders of the principle of voluntarism are going through a kind of wilderness experience today. This is the cost of abandoning the fleshpots of Egypt. No more leeks, onions, garlic, and Federal handouts. Perhaps no more tax exemption, as the warfare escalates. Perhaps even a bit of persecution. But the early church received no tax exemptions. Luther did not train future Lutheran ministers by means of vouchers for seminary education issued by the Vatican, either. The lack of such support slows down the development of a movement in its early stages, when it is learning to cope with the realities of life, but sparse beginnings enable it to deal with growth and success later on, when its principles become more widely accepted.

GRASS-ROOTS ORGANIZATIONS

"Organizations": The word is plural, not singular. The idea of establishing a single grass-roots organization is preposterous. It would be mowed down by the wide-blade power mowers of the opposition as soon as its sprouts were detected. Multiple organizations, on the other hand, can affect changes in many places, especially out of the way places where the opposition does not have its wide-blade mowers available.

Men try out different types of grass in different environments. In one place it may be Bermuda grass (or Bahamas grass, or even Switzerland grass). In others it may be plain old crab grass. What it must not be is unwatered, unfertilized grass that will wither when the mid-day sun hits it. That is the grass which humanists have planted, and as the State's restraints on freedom squeeze productivity out of the legal, visible markets, the end of cheap Federal fertilizers and cheap water will lead to a cnange in ownership of the field.

Wnat we have is exactly what we need: *alternative grass seeds*, hidden from view in minor and seemingly insignificant fields. We are steadily raising up new, non-hybrid "seeds" that will survive the competition of new blights and new environments. The hybrid seed used by the State produces a lush lawn, but only under limited environmental conditions and only by continually returning to the monopolistic hybrid seed sellers. It is not a resilient variety of grass.

Grass-roots organizations are all around us. Not one; many. They may co-operate with others for limited ends, but they have their own timetables, resources, and goals. They are competitive. Not all will survive; some will. Those that do survive will replace the existing structures of society, all over the world. Humanism is a worldwide phenomenon; it will collapse as a worldwide phenomenon, to be replaced by numerous biblical-cultural alternatives.

CONCLUSION The apparent ineffectiveness of small, underfunded ideological or religious organizations is deceptive. All long-term social change comes from the successful efforts of one or another struggling organization to capture the minds of a hard core of future leaders, as well as the respect of a wider population. There is no other way to change a society. The hope of stepping into power overnight without planning is naive, let alone the hope of getting financial support from the existing leadership.

The Hebrews of Joshua's generation wandered in the wilderness for 40 years until their parents died. They had to prepare themselves mentally and organizationally for the battle to come. They certainly did not bother to court the favor of the king of Jericho, nor did they worry too much that the Levites had not graduated from fully accredited Baal Theological Seminary. If we only recognized our wilderness condition for what it is, we might not continue to make the mistakes in strategy that the Hebrews of Joshua's day didn't make.

CONCLUSION

". . . the steady, thoughtful, informed presentation of a biblical vision of victory will eventually produce converts."

This book is both educational and motivational. If you have agreed with its overall perspective, then you owe it to yourself, your fellow Christians, the world around you, and most of all to God, to begin to rethink your theology. You have an obligation to determine for yourself whether or not you are responsible to begin a personal program of Christian reconstruction, beginning with your own daily affairs, and continuing for the rest of your life. And if you have this responsibility, then other Christians have it, too. Will you help them to come to grips with this responsibility by telling them what you have learned? Will you help to encourage your fellow church members to step forth and take a stand for the crown rights of King Jesus?

Where should you begin? With the Bible. Sit down and begin a systematic study of the Bible, from Genesis to Revelation. Get one or two modern translations to help you understand what the Bible requires. Ask yourself, over and over, verse by verse: "What does this mean, and how does it apply to today's society?" Try to make sense out of God's word. This may require the purchase of Bible commentaries and other study guides, but it must be done. Little people have to do it. Then begin to share your thoughts tentatively. See if others are interested in finding out what God's word requires for every area of life. Maybe you should set up a study group. Maybe your church would be willing to co-operate. (Then again, maybe not.) If you can get more than one person involved, you begin to make use of the intellectual division of labor.

Start subscribing to newsletters that explain some of these biblical passages in the light of today's world. I am not referring to prophecy. I am referring to biblical law. Read my introductory book, *Unconditional Surrender: God's Program for Victory* (2nd ed.; Tyler, Texas: Geneva Divinity School Press, 1983: $9.95). Read R. J. Rushdoony's *Institutes of Biblical Law* (P.O. Box 817, Phillipsburg, New Jersey: Presbyterian and Reformed Publishing Company $24). Subscribe to all of the following newsletter and newspaper services:

Institute for Christian Economics
P.O. Box 8000
Tyler, TX 75711

Geneva Divinity School
708 Hamvasy Ln.
Tyler, TX 75701

Chalcedon Report   Christian News
P.O. Box 158   P.O. Box 168
Vallecito, CA 95251   New Haven, MO 63068

You will at first encounter a wall of resistance. Count on it. But the steady, thoughtful, informed presentation of a biblical vision of victory will eventually produce converts. Others will begin to see some of the implications of what you are talking about. You will experience success, but not if you sit on your hands and do nothing.

If nothing else, buy spare copies of this book and begin to lend them out. Lend them out with a *specific time limit*, preferably a week or two. Ask the other person to report back and tell you what he thinks about it. Get together to discuss it. He may have insights that you missed. But the important thing is to see if the message in this book strikes a responsive chord in the heart of another person. If it does, you have become the first two members of a Christian Reconstruction Bible study group.

Bible lectures are informative, but a true *discussion* group should probably not be larger than three people. Three people can really discuss in detail. Also, the presence of a third person tends to reduce the likelihood of intense discussions (also known as shouting matches) between two members.

Your goal is to begin a group. Each member should do his best to recruit two people for a new group. Thus, each member ideally spends one hour per week with the group which first recruited him, and one hour with the group he recruited. A Christian Reconstruction Bible study is not to become any sort of initiatory secret society. But a tightly knit, highly personal, three-person group is just a good way to spread the message.

These meetings will not eat up a person's time, because members agree in advance never to continue the meetings beyond one hour. This allows each member (along with spouses and other affected persons) to plan his day in terms of a *predictable* schedule for Bible discussions. If people indulge themselves and spend additional hours in unplanned discussions, someone will grow resentful: members of the group, spouses, children of participants, or others who are in some way dependent on the participants. Warning: Christian Reconstruction Bible studies already have enough people upset at the basic idea of broad Christian responsibility; there is no use in creating additional resentment.

Each discussion group member, after about six months, should begin recruiting his own group. Take what you have learned over half a year of study and begin to teach others. Get the division of labor going. Don't rush into a leadership position until you are fairly confident that you will not embarrass yourself or the word of God. But don't hesitate forever, searching for perfection. Start small. Despise not the day of small beginnings.

It may be that you are not ready to begin a discussion group. Maybe you just don't have the time to read more newsletters. Maybe Bible reading is a chore for you. Perhaps you are just too busy making a living or whatever to devote time to a consideration of your responsibilities before God.

If so, please do yourself a favor. Don't throw this book away. Put it on the shelf and keep it in the back of your mind. When the crisis comes, get it off the shelf and reread it.

"What crisis?" you may ask. The one which always comes to those who know what they are required by God to do, but refuse to do it. "Therefore to him that knoweth to do good, and doeth it not, to him it is sin" (James 4:17). You have been warned about your comprehensive responsibilities. There is no going back. For all eternity, there is no going back. Whether you are required to start a study group is not the question. What is relevant is the question of your efforts to redeem the time—literally, to buy it back. What is relevant is for you to begin your efforts at bringing your portion of the world under the visible sovereignty of biblical law.

GLOSSARY

Some of the terminology presented in this book may be unfamiliar to many people. A brief glossary showing how I am using the words may be helpful.

CHRISTIAN RECONSTRUCTION A recently articulated philosophy which argues that it is the moral obligation of Christians to recapture every institution for Jesus Christ. It proclaims "the crown rights of King Jesus." The means by which this task might be accomplished — a few CR's are not convinced that it can be — is biblical law. This is the "tool of dominion." We have been assigned a *dominion covenant* — a God-given assignment to men to conquer in His name (Gen. 1:28; 9:1-7). The founders of the movement have combined four basic Christian beliefs into one overarching system: 1) biblical law, 2) optimistic eschatology, 3) predestination (providence), and 4) presuppositional apologetics (philosophical defense of the faith). Not all CR's hold all four positions, but the founders have held all four. The first person who put this system together publicly was Rousas John Rushdoony. He was my mentor during the 1960's, and while I was working on the specific field of economics, he was developing the overall framework. The first comprehensive introduction to the Christian Reconstruction position was Rushdoony's *The Institutes of Biblical Law* (Craig Press, 1973), in which three of my appendices appear. The easiest introduction to the position is my book, *Unconditional Surrender: God's Program for Victory* (2nd ed., Geneva Divinity School Press, 1983).

DOOYEWEERDIANISM A philosophy pioneered by the Dutch Calvinist legal philosopher, Herman Dooyeweerd (DOUGH-yeh-vehrd), in the mid-twentieth century. His major work is *A New Critique of Theoretical Thought*. He argued with considerable erudition (and appalling verbiage) that there is no neutrality in any philosophical system. All philosophies and outlooks rely on what he called *pre-theoretical assumptions* about man, nature, law, and God. His shorter book, *In the Twilight of Western Thought*, presents a 3-part outline of Western philosophy. He categorically rejected the idea that biblical revelation can provide either the categories of philosophy or the content of Christian philosophy. His system therefore lends itself to various "common ground" appeals to the universally logical mind of man. Many of his younger followers have turned to some variation of socialism, most commonly medieval guild socialism, as an answer to the perceived evils of humanistic Communism and humanistic capitalism. The movement centers in a large home in Toronto, Canada, which was made a graduate studies center in the mid-1960's. The influence of this movement peaked, 1965-75.

ESCHATOLOGY The doctrine of "the last things." It refers to the second (or third) coming of Jesus Christ. There are three major schools of eschatology: premillennialism, amillennialism, and postmillennialism. The "pre," "a," and "post" refer to the timing of Christ's return in relation to the millennium, an age of Christian victory.

The *pre*millennialist believes that Jesus will return in person to set up an earthly kingdom a thousand years before the final judgment. Thus, Christ comes *pre*millennially — *before* the millennium. A major dispute has divided premillennialists for 160 years: the question of a period, if any, between Christ's return to "gather His saints in the air" to transform them into perfect beings, and their return to earth with him to rule. *Pre*-tribulation dispensationalists say there will be a seven-year interlude, during which the Great Tribulation will come upon the earth, especially on a rebuilt national Israel in Palestine. *Post*-tribulation dispensationalists say that the seven-year Tribulation comes before Christ's premillennial return to gather the saints. The church will "go through the meat-grinder," in other words. There has been a revival of post-tribulation dispensationalism since about 1973. *Historic* premillennialism, represented best in our era by George Eldon

Ladd, is *post*-tribulationist, but argues that there are only two dispensations, Old and New. This was the common premillennial view from the early church until the 1820's.

The *a*millennialist argues that the millennium is totally spiritual in nature, not external, and refers to the church age. Thus, there will never be an earthly victory for Christians before the return of Jesus at the final judgment. The Dutch Calvinist tradition, the Lutheran tradition, and the Roman Catholic tradition are all amillennial in outlook.

The *post*millennialist argues that Jesus will come in final judgment *after* a long era of peace—peace that is the product of the universal domination of Christians and Christian institutions across the face of the earth. John Calvin was usually "post," but sometimes "a." Historically, the Puritans were the most influential postmillennialists, especially the New England Puritans of the first generation, 1630-60. Jonathan Edwards was also postmillennial, as were many of his followers. There was a strong postmillennial undercurrent during the years preceding the American Revolution. The Presbyterians, North and South, were postmillennial—the Southern church until the South lost the Civil War (War Between the States) in 1865; the Northern church right up until the First World War. Humanists in the churches secularized the postmillennial vision, from 1830 onward, and ever since the era of the Social Gospel (1870's), fundamentalists have asserted repeatedly that postmillennialism means theological liberalism. But it wasn't liberal before the Arminian revivalists and then the Unitarians reworked its framework to conform with newer theological trends in the United States.

The Christian Reconstruction movement has been developed primarily by postmillennialists since the late 1960's, but many of the premises of the CR position have been enthusiastically adopted by premillennialists. A handful of Dutch amillennialists believe in the principle of Christian Reconstruction; they just don't believe we can ever pull it off before the day of judgment.

FUNDAMENTALISM The word was first used by a liberal critic, Harry Emerson Fosdick, in the early 1920's. He was referring to theological conservatives. A mass-circulation series of 12 booklets by Christian scholars, *The Fundamentals*, had been sent to 300,000 pastors, missionaries, and Sunday School teachers, beginning around 1910. (These are still in print in a 4-volume set published by Baker Book House in Grand Rapids, Michigan.) It was common to define the fundamentalist faith by means of a series of creedal statements: 1) the verbal, plenary inspiration of the Bible; 2) the divinity of Jesus Christ; 3) the virgin birth; 4) the historical reality of miracles; and 5) the second coming of Christ in judgment. But additional aspects of the social and cultural views of the fundamentalists narrowed the definition (and excluded others who held to the first five positions, e.g., Lutherans, Presbyterians, and, for that matter, Roman Catholics): 1) total abstinence from alcohol (also dancing, moving pictures, and tobacco); 2) disdain for (or fear of) higher education generally; 3) disengagement from politics, especially after 1925; 4) an increasing concentration on the physical return of Jesus Christ to establish a personal thousand-year reign on earth, prior to the final judgment (i.e., premillennial dispensationalism). A good introduction to the subject is George Marsden's *Fundamentalism and American Culture* (Oxford University Press, 1980), which covers the period 1870-1925.

HUMANISM   This philosophy maintains that "man is the measure of all things," a phrase attributed to the presocratic Greek philosopher, Protagoras (about 450 B.C.). The Roman poet Terence said, "I am a man, and nothing human is foreign to me." (The founder of Communism, Karl Marx, was fond of this phrase.) The basic philosophy of humanism is that there is no God-created standard of judgment outside of man by which men may be judged or changed. Man either creates his own standards (a more common view since 1859, when Charles Darwin's *On the Origin of Species* was published), or discovers the "natural" (uncreated) laws of nature and human society (an older, pre-Darwinian viewpoint). *Secular humanism* is a more consistent variant which categorically denies any sort of God who might intervene in the affairs (especially ethical affairs) of mankind. It is more straightforwardly atheistic and aggressive against religion in general and Bible-based Christianity in particular.

LAW-ORDER   Another term for the comprehensive law structure of the Bible. This is a coherent system of law which applies to every area of man's life. It is this law structure which provides man with his "tool of dominion." Law gives men the standards of personal action, including their relations with each other, nature, and God. A law-order is an inescapable concept. It is never a question of law or no law. It is a question of *whose* law. Either the law of God is the ethical standard of all human affairs, or else some rival law structure is. In short, there is no neutral ethics, no neutral morality, and therefore no neutral law-order.

The opposite of biblical law is *antinomianism*, which invariably produces tyranny, for it leaves man unprotected by God's law. The State or the Church become tyrannical, since they become more and more consistent to their philosophy that there is no God-revealed law-order to restrain them.

Biblical law cannot save man from sin, but it does offer him guidelines for reconstructing the world to conform to God's standards (social ethics), just as it provides redeemed men with guidelines for personal ethics. We are not under law as a death-dealing judge, but we *are* under law as a standard of performance. "By their fruits ye shall know them," Jesus said. Christians are under law as grace-protected, grace-redeemed people.

Fundamentalists whose doctrine of salvation and doctrine of eschatology are both antinomian—"We're under grace, not law"—have in the past denied the continuing applicability of Old Testament law in the church age. Leaders of the "new fundamentalism" have attempted to return to biblical law through the back door by using such terms as "biblical principles," or "biblical ethics," or "the moral standards of the Bible." But if the principles are morally binding, they must be regarded as *laws*.

If there is no neutrality anywhere in the universe, and biblical standards apply universally, then all academic disciplines of the modern university are to be governed by biblical revelation and biblical law. On this point, see the book which I edited, *Foundations of Christian Scholarship* (Ross House Books, P.O. Box 67, Vallecito, CA 95251).

LIBERATION THEOLOGY Popular among liberals in all denominations, liberation theology adopts the language of socialist wealth redistribution, Marxist revolutionary rhetoric, and out-of-context Bible quotes. It has become extremely popular in Latin America among radical Roman Catholic clerics. It has also swept through the "neo-evangelical" community. Not all of its adherents are openly revolutionary. Some of them are vague. Others are chicken. Baptist theologian Ronald Sider is probably best classified as a non-revolutionary liberation theologian (as of early 1985). His book, *Rich Christians in an Age of Hunger*, was co-published by the liberal Roman Catholic Paulist Press and the neo-evangelical InterVarsity Press. The best refutation of liberation theology by a Protestant (or anyone else, for that matter), is David Chilton's *Productive Christians in an Age of Guilt-Manipulators* (3rd ed., Institute for Christian Economics, 1985). It is also the best introduction to Christian economics.

PRESUPPOSITIONALISM This term refers generally to any philosophy which argues that the conclusions men draw from all evidence is governed by their operating presuppositions concerning God, man, law, and nature. More specifically, the term refers to the writings of the Dutch-American Calvinist philosopher, Cornelius Van Til, who is still alive as I write these words. His major books include *Christianity and Barthianism*, *The New Modernism*, *The Defense of the Faith*, and *A Christian Theory of Knowledge*. He is generally regarded as the "patron philosopher," if not the patron saint, of the Christian Reconstruction movement. Van Til categorically denies all applications of the idea of neutrality, which is at root a philosophy of the self-proclaimed autonomous man. In contrast to Dooyeweerd, Van Til has always argued that the Bible provides both the framework (categories) and content of Christian philosophy. He never pursued this thesis with respect to specific biblical revelation concerning biblical law, a task which was taken up by his disciple, R. J. Rushdoony, especially in *The Institutes of Biblical Law*, and by a younger disciple of Van Til, Greg L. Bahnsen (*Theonomy in Christian Ethics*).

SYNCRETISM An application of the doctrine of neutralism. It is a mixed philosophy which attempts to combine biblical revelation with the insights of human philosophy, most notably Greek philosophy. This characterizes the philosophy of the medieval Roman Catholic scholar, Thomas Aquinas ("Thomism"). It also characterizes the philosophical defenses of the faith offered by Lutherans and almost all other Protestants, including fundamentalists. Such a defense usually involves four or five "proofs of God" that supposedly demonstrate the inescapable nature of God — though not a God who possesses all of the characteristics specifically revealed in the Bible.

Van Til is the most important critic of syncretism. He says that if we begin with the presupposition that fallen man's mind is logically capable of coming to faith in a god, then that god cannot possibly be the God of the Bible. The God of the Bible has revealed to men in His word that all the earth is totally dependent on Him, the Creator and Sustainer of the universe. Therefore, man is not autonomous, and man's speculations are not autonomous. We must start with the presupposition of God and His revelation, or else we cannot logically end with such a God. If we start with the logic of autonomous man, then the "god" produced or discovered by autonomous man's mind cannot be the omnipotent God of the Bible. Thus, all attempts to mix Christianity with autonomous man's philosophies must result in the abandonment of biblical Christianity.

Two introductions to Van Til's thought are R. J. Rushdoony's *By What Standard?* (Thoburn Press, P.O. Box 6941, Tyler, TX 75711, and Richard Pratt *Every Thought Captive* (Presbyterian and Reformed Publishing Company, P.O. Box 817, Phillipsburg, NJ 08865).

SCRIPTURE INDEX

INDEX

Unconditional Surrender: God's Program for Victory

Gary North

There is a war on. The war is between God and Satan. In our day, we see it most clearly in the conflicts between Christian institutions and the institutions of secular humanism. It is a war that is not going to go away. There will be a winner.

Unconditional Surrender is an introduction to this conflict. It covers the fundamental issues of the war: 1) What is the nature of *God*? 2) What is the nature of *man*? 3) What is the nature of *law*? If we can begin to answer these questions, then we will be able to recognize the nature of the battle.

Does Christianity make a difference in life? Does Christianity offer real-life solutions to the basic issues of life? Unquestionably, the answer is *yes*. But if we answer in the affirmative, then we have to start getting specific. Exactly how does Christianity make a difference? What kind of society would Christianity bring forth? In what ways would such a society be different from the society we live in today, the society of humanism? Is there a specifically biblical system of social ethics? What *practical* difference should Christianity make in the life of a ruler, businessman, judge, teacher, or scientist?

This book introduces people to the fundamentals of Christianity, including *applied* Christianity. It is thoroughly biblical. It provides evidence taken directly from the Scriptures. It offers suggestions for further reading, as well as the names and addresses of independent Christian organizations that are equipping Christians for the battles they face today.

264 pp., indexed, bibliography, pb., $9.95
Geneva Ministries
P.O. Box 8376, Tyler, TX 75711

75 Bible Questions Your Instructors Pray You Won't Ask

Gary North

Unless you're "one in ten thousand" as Christians go, you've been misled. Maybe it hasn't been deliberate on the part of your Bible teachers, but it's true. In Christian college classrooms, pulpits, and Sunday Schools throughout the land, people are being misinformed about Christianity, year after year.

Subtitled *How to Spot Humanism in the Classroom or Pulpit*, this hard-hitting little volume of pointed questions exposes many of the doctrinal compromises which modern Christian leaders are making with currently popular forms of Baal worship. People who think they are hearing "the good, old-time religion" are being indoctrinated by well-meaning (and sometimes not so well-meaning) teachers who are either outright humanists or who have been compromised by some of humanism's most important doctrines.

75 Bible Questions covers three crucial battlefields in the war between Christianity and humanism:

1. Sovereignty: God's or Man's?
2. Law: God's or Man's?
3. Kingdom: God's or Man's?

Warning: This is probably the most controversial Christian book you will ever read. Some humanist/Christian colleges would expel a student for even owning a copy. Packed with Scripture references and helpful suggestions about organizing study groups, this valuable book also contains special sections on how to stay out of trouble while reading it. *75 Bible Questions* will change your thinking—permanently!

300 pp., appendices, bibliography, pb., $4.95
Spurgeon Press
P.O. Box 7999, Tyler, TX 75711

Paradise Restored: A Biblical Theology of Dominion

David Chilton

In recent years many Christians have begun to realize a long forgotten truth: God wants us to have dominion over the earth, just as He originally commanded Adam and Eve. By His atonement, Jesus Christ has restored us to Adam's lost position, guaranteeing that God's original plan will be fulfilled. God will be glorified throughout the world: *"The earth shall be full of the knowledge of the LORD, as the waters cover the sea." Isaiah 11:9.*

In order to demonstrate this truth from Scripture, David Chilton begins at the beginning, in the Garden of Eden. He shows how God established basic patterns in the first few chapters of Genesis—patterns which form the structure of later Biblical revelation. In the course of this book on eschatology, the reader is treated to an exciting, refreshingly *Biblical* way of reading the Bible. Avoiding the pitfalls of speculation, Chilton shows how even the most obscure prophecies can suddenly come alive with meaning to those who have grasped the Paradise Theme.

Building on a solid foundation of New Testament eschatology, the author deals at length with the message of the Book of Revelation—often with surprising results. Throughout the volume, the reader is confronted with the fact that our view of the *future* is inescapably bound up with our view of *Jesus Christ*. According to the author, the fact that Jesus is *now* King of kings and Lord of lords means that His Gospel must be victorious· the Holy Spirit will bring the water of life to the ends of the earth. The Christian message is one of Hope. Christ has defeated the devil, and we can look forward to increasing triumphs for His Kingdom in this age. Pentecost was just the beginning.

352 pp., indexed, bibliography, hb., $14.95
Dominion Press
P.O. Box 8204, Ft. Worth, TX 76124

Productive Christians in an Age of Guilt-Manipulators

David Chilton

One of the most insidious attacks upon orthodox Christianity has come from the so-called "Christian Left." This book answers the "bible" of that movement, *Rich Christians in an Age of Hunger*, by Ronald Sider.

David Chilton demonstrates that the "Christian Socialism" advocated by Sider is nothing more than baptized humanism—the goal of which is not charity, but raw, police-state power.

The debate between Sider and Chilton centers on one central issue: *Does the Bible have clear guidelines for every area of life?* Sider claims that the Bible does not contain "blueprints" for a social and economic order. The catch, of course, is that Sider then provides *his own* "blueprints" for society, calling for a taxation system which is completely condemned by God's infallible word. Chilton answers that the socialist "cure" is worse than the disease, for socialism actually *increases* poverty. Even when motivated by good intentions, unbiblical "charity" programs will damage the very people they seek to help.

Combining incisive satire with hard-hitting argumentation and extensive biblical references, Chilton shows that the Bible *does* have clear, forthright, and workable answers to the problem of poverty. *Productive Christians* is most importantly a major introduction to the system of Christian Economics, with chapters on biblical law, welfare, poverty, the third world, overpopulation, foreign aid, advertising, profits, and economic growth.

458 pp., indexed, bibliography, pb., $12.50
Institute for Christian Economics
P.O. Box 8000, Tyler, TX 75711

The Law of the Covenant: An Exposition of Exodus 21-23

James B. Jordan

How relevant are the laws of the Old Testament for today? God said that Israel was to be a light to the nations (Isaiah 42:6). That someday all nations would come to Jerusalem to receive the Law (Micah 4:2). That in His Law, "every transgression and disobedience receives a just recompense" (Hebrews 2:2). That all peoples would marvel at the wisdom and justice of Israel's laws (Deuteronomy 4:6-8).

Yet, with the change from the Old to the New Covenant, there are clearly changes in the Law, "for when the priesthood changes, there must also take place a change of law" (Hebrews 7:12). How, then, are we to approach the many laws found in the Old Testament? Do they apply to Christians? If so, how?

In this book, Mr. Jordan provides four introductory chapters on the nature of Biblical law, on the redemptive historical context in which the law was first written, and on the overall changes in the law system which the New Covenant brings. Then, moving to the concrete, Mr. Jordan provides the first truly in-depth commentary on the case laws of Exodus 21-23, the Book of the Covenant. The laws are taken up one at a time. In each case, the question is asked, "What did this law mean to the people of the Old Testament age?" Then the question is asked, "What relevance might this law have for the Christian faith today?" Finally, the question is asked, "How does this law shed light on the work of Jesus Christ, of whom all Scripture speaks? That is, how can we preach Christ from this law?"

In his preface, Mr. Jordan states that he has not tried to say the last word on these chapters of Scripture, but that he has tried to say a first word, and to challenge the Church to look further into these verses to find wisdom for today. No preacher and no student of the Word can afford to be without this study.

310 pp., indexed, hb., $17.50
Institute for Christian Economics
P.O. Box 8000, Tyler, TX 75711

Moses and Pharaoh: Dominion Religion Versus Power Religion

Gary North

In the fifteenth century before the birth of Jesus, Moses came before Pharaoh and made what seemed to be a minor request: Pharaoh should allow the Israelites to make a three-day journey in order to sacrifice to their God. But this was not a minor request; given the theology of Egypt, *it was the announcement of a revolution*—an anti-humanist revolution.

The conflict between Moses and Pharaoh was a conflict between the religion of the Bible and its rival, the religion of humanism. It is not common for scholars to identify Egypt's polytheism with modern humanism, but the two theologies share their most fundamental doctrines: the irrelevance of the God of the Bible for the affairs of men; the evolution of man into God; the impossibility of an infallible word of God; the nonexistence of permanent laws of God; the impossibility of temporal judgment by God; and a belief in the power of man.

What Bible commentators have failed to understand is that the conflict between Moses and Pharaoh was at heart a conflict between the two major religions in man's history, *dominion religion* and *power religion*, with the third major religion—*escapist religion*—represented by the Hebrew slaves. What they have also failed to point out is that *there is an implicit alliance between the power religion and the escapist religion*. This alliance still exists.

This book is a detailed study of the conflict between Moses and Pharaoh. It discusses the implications of this conflict in several areas: theology, politics, sociology, and especially economics. This book is Part One of the second volume of a multi-volume set, *An Economic Commentary on the Bible*. The first volume, *The Dominion Covenant: Genesis*, was published in 1982.

432 pp., indexed, pb., $12.50
Institute for Christian Economics,
P.O. Box 8000, Tyler, TX 75711

Christian News
P.O. Box 168
New Haven, MO 63068

Gentlemen:

   Gary North mentions you newspaper in his book, *Backward, Christian Soldiers?* Please send me a copy.

_____
name

_____
address

_____
city, state, zip

Rev. R. J. Rushdoony
Chalcedon
P.O. Box 158
Vallecito, CA 95251

Dear Rev. Rushdoony:

   Gary North in his paperback book, *Backward, Christian
Soldiers?*, suggests that I would be interested in the newsletter you publish. I want to sign up for a subscription to
your monthly newsletter, *The Chalcedon Report*. Thank
you.

_____
name

_____
address

_____
city, state, zip

☐ Enclosed is a tax-deductible donation to help
   meet expenses.

WHY IS THIS
TEAR-OUT SHEET
STILL IN THIS BOOK?

Tear-out sheets are supposed
to be torn out and mailed in.

STOP
PROCRASTINATING!

Freedom Council
CBN Television
Virginia Beach, VA 23466

Gentlemen:

I read about your organization in Gary North's book,
Backward, Christian Soldiers? Please send me information on
how I can get involved in politics as a Christian.

_____
name

_____
address

_____
city, state, zip

Rev. Paul Lindstrom, Superintendent of Schools
Christian Liberty Academy Satellite Schools
203 East Camp McDonald Road
Prospect Heights, IL 60070

Dear Rev. Lindstrom:

Gary North in his paperback book, *Backward, Christian
Soldiers?*, suggests that I would be interested in the Christian Liberty Academy Satellite Schools program (CLASS).
Please send me your free information packet that shows
how parents can provide their children with a good education using your traditional, Christian, conservative
oriented program.

_____
name

_____
address

_____
city, state, zip

☐ Enclosed is a donation to help meet expenses.

WHY IS THIS
TEAR-OUT SHEET
STILL IN THIS BOOK?

Tear-out sheets are supposed
to be torn out and mailed in.

STOP
PROCRASTINATING!

Plymouth Rock Foundation
P.O. Box 425
Marlborough, NH 03455

Gentlemen:

Gary North in his paperback book, *Backward, Christian Soldiers?*, suggests that I would like to know more about your Foundation and its programs and publications and what it is doing "to advance the kingdom of The Lord Jesus Christ." Please send me an information packet and place me on your mailing list for a trial subscription to your periodicals, the *Letter from Plymouth Rock* and the *FAC-Sheet*.

_____
name

_____
address

_____
city, state, zip

☐ I am also interested in knowing about FUNDAMENTALS FOR AMERICAN CHRISTIANS, your study course in Biblical Principles of Self and Civil Government.

☐ I would like to know about your seminars on the Principle Approach to Christian education.

☐ Enclosed is a tax-deductible donation to help meet expenses.

- -

Gary North
Dominion Seminars
P.O. Box 8204
Ft. Worth, TX 76124

Dear Dr. North:

Our church may be interested in bringing in one of your seminars on "Christian Survival on the Secular Campus." Please send us information on this seminar program.

_____
name

_____
church

_____
address

_____
city, state, zip

WHY IS THIS
TEAR-OUT SHEET
STILL IN THIS BOOK?

Tear-out sheets are supposed
to be torn out and mailed in.

STOP
PROCRASTINATING!

Geneva Ministries
P.O. Box 131300
Tyler, TX 75713

Gentlemen:

  I read about your newsletters in Gary North's
Backward, Christian Soldiers? Please send me a sample
packet of materials

_____
name

_____
address

_____
city, state, zip

☐ I'm enclosing a tax-deductible donation to help
   defray expenses.

WHY IS THIS
TEAR-OUT SHEET
STILL IN THIS BOOK?

Tear-out sheets are supposed
to be torn out and mailed in.

STOP
PROCRASTINATING!

Dr. Gary North
Institute for Christian Economics
P.O. Box 8000
Tyler, TX 75711

Dear Dr. North:

I read about your organization in your book, *Backward, Christian Soldiers?* I understand that you publish several newsletters that are sent out for six months free of charge. I would be interested in receiving them:

☐ *Biblical Economics Today, Dominion Strategies,* and *Christian Reconstruction*

Please send any other information you have concerning your program.

_____
name

_____
address

_____
city, state, zip

☐ I'm enclosing a tax-deductible donation to help defray expenses.

WHY IS THIS
TEAR-OUT SHEET
STILL IN THIS BOOK?

Tear-out sheets are supposed
to be torn out and mailed in.

STOP
PROCRASTINATING!